RAPID RESULTS Credit Repair Credit Dispute Letter System

John D. Harris

My Experience: Finance Degree, 6 years loans officer at a national bank, 4 1/2 years credit bureau manager for one of the big three credit bureau's   John Harris

Contents

LET'S GET STARTED 1
THINGS I NEED YOU TO DO BEFORE WE START WITH THE REPAIR PROCESS 2
WHAT IS CREDIT 4
History of Credit 5
Credit in Early America 6
HISTORY OF CREDIT CARDS 8
The Main Axis Players 12
The Credit Bureaus also known as Credit Reporting Agencies (CRA's), Data Furnishers and FICO 12
First Let's Look at Credit Reporting Agencies (CRA's) 13
There Are Three Credit Reporting Agencies (CRA's) 13
TransUnion Equifax and Experian In Depth 15
Experian In Depth 15
Equifax In Depth 16
TransUnion In Depth 19
Things You Should Know About The Credit Bureaus 20
All the Credit Reporting Agencies Have Different Reports On You 21
Credit Reporting Agencies Are NOT Government Agencies 21
How do Credit Reporting Agencies Make Money 21
Four Data Products Sold by Credit Bureaus 22
The Data Furnishers 23
Where do the Credit Reporting Agencies Get the information 23
Data Furnishers Are Required By The FCRA Fair Credit Reporting Act (More About This Later) to Comply With These Regulations 25
Guidelines for Data Furnishers Policies and Procedures from FCRC 25
DISPUTES 28
ADDITIONAL RESPONSIBILITIES 30
FICO 31

ii

Why FICO?	31
How Does FICO Make Money?	33
Definition of *proprietary*	33
How is your Credit Score (FICO) calculated	33
More FICO Scores	35
Why All The Different FICOS?	35
Interesting FICO Score Information	37
The Newest FICO Score....Drum Roll Please .....FICO 9	37
VantageScore	39
New Advantages of VantageScore 3.0	40
VantageScore vs FICO	40
FICO / VantageScore Differences	41
Other Credit Scores	42
YOUR ALLIES THE FTC	43
The "Fair Credit Reporting Act"	44
Consumer Reports	44
The FCRA Regulates	45
Users of Consumer Reports	45
Employment Background checks	45
Furnishers of Information	46
Consumer Reporting Agencies	47
Nationwide Specialty Consumer Reporting Agencies	47
YOUR OTHER ALLIES THE BK BOMB	48
Should You Claim Bankruptcy	49
Things To Consider	50
How Do You Claim Bankruptcy	50
Chapter 7 Bankruptcy	51
Chapter 13 Bankruptcy	51
What Can You Dismiss in a Bankruptcy	52
What Can't You Dismiss in Bankruptcy	52
The Basic of Credit Card Debt and Bankruptcy	53
Credit Card Debt is Dischargeable in Bankruptcy	53
Fraud Will Prevent Credit Card Debt From Being Discharged	54
Can You Keep a Credit Card Out of Your Bankruptcy	54
Will You Be Able to Get a Credit Card After Bankruptcy	54
How Will Bankruptcy Effect Your Credit	55

My Experience: Finance Degree, 6 years loans officer at a national bank, 4 1/2 years credit bureau manager for one of the big three credit bureau's   John Harris

How Long Will Bankruptcy Effect Your Credit 55
Not Your Ally 56
Debt Consolidation 56
Red Flags that Indicate a Debt Consolidation Scam 57
Choose a Legitimate Debt Consolidation Loan Program 58
Getting Your Reports and Scores 59
The Annualcreditreport JOKE 59
Here Again Let's See What The FTC Says About This Site 59
Credit Monitoring 61
More Allies CreditKarma.com 62
Why Use CreditKarma.com? 62
What's the Catch? 62
More Catches 63
Getting Your Experian Credit Report FreeCreditReport.com 63
https://www.creditsesame.com/ 64
www.equifax.com/personal/ 64
MyFico.com 64
PrivacyGuard.com 65
CreditCheckTotal.com 65
Free Fico/Vantage Scores 66
Credit Report and Score Must Do's 69
Credit Bureaus Are Always Gaming You 69
TransUnion's Forced Arbitration Terms of Service 70
Equifax's Forced Arbitration Terms of Service 71
Experian's Forced Arbitration Terms of Service 72
Opt-Out of Forced Arbitration 76
Identification Form: 77
Identification Form Requirements 78
Contacting the Bureau Requirements 78
Opt-Out Letter 79
Now Get it Notarized 80

- *Opt-Out Addresses* 80
- *Now Track Your letters* 81
- *What's on Your Credit Report* 81
- *Identifying Information* 81
- *Trade Lines* 82
- *Credit Inquiries* 82
- *Public Record and Collections* 82
- *What's Not on Your Credit Report* 82
- *Prepaid Debit Cards, Checking Accounts and Debit Cards* 82
- *Evidence That You Are Now Married* 83
- *Wealth Metrics* 84
- *Public Utilities* 84
- *Categories On Your Credit Report* 85
- *Categories-Public Records* 85
- *Bankruptcy* 85
- *Tax Lien* 86
- *Civil Judgements* 86
- *Great News About Public Records* 86
- *NCAP Settlement Details* 87
- *More Great NCAP News* 87
- *Bankruptcy The Last Public Record Standing* 89
- *Categories-Credit Inquiries* 90
- *Hard and Soft Inquiries* 90
- *Inquiries Are Removed After 2 Years* 91
- *How Do Inquiries Affect Your Credit Score* 91
- *Top Secret Fico Point System For Hard Inquiries* 91
- *Categories-Collection Accounts* 92
- *Going Into Collections* 93
- *Collections Step by Step* 93
- *How Long Do Collections Stay on Your Report* 95
- *How Collections Impact Your Credit Report* 95
- *Will Paying My Collection Accounts Increase My Score* 95
- *Categories- Accounts* 96
- *Categories- Adverse Accounts, Potentially Negative Items* 97
- *Fixing Your Credit* 98
- *Identifying* 98

My Experience: Finance Degree, 6 years loans officer at a national bank, 4 1/2 years credit bureau manager for one of the big three credit bureau's   John Harris

Adding Points 98
Deleting Negatives 98
Identifying 98
Step 1 99
Step 2 100
Step 3A Inquiries 100
Step 3B Public Records and Collections 102
Step 3C Bad Accounts 104
Step 3D Bad Addresses 106
Step 4 Repeat the Process for Equifax 106
Step 5 Repeat the Process for Experian 106
Adding Points 107
Adding Points by Not Losing Points 107
Don't Pay Your Bills Late From This Day Forward 107
Don't Co-Sign on Debt 108
Add Rent to Your Credit Report 108
Rent Track 111
Add All Your Good Standing Accounts To All Your Reports 111
Sample Add Account Letter 112
Identification Form: 113
Identification Form Requirements 115
Contacting the Bureau Requirements 115
Now Track Your letters 115
Paying Off The Wrong Debt 116
Add 1 or Preferably 2- Low Amount Secured Loans 116
SelfLender.com 117
Second Secured Loan 117
Department Store Cards UGH 118
The Almighty Credit Card 119
Having No Credit Cards 119
How Many Cards Should You Have 120

Getting Secured Credit Cards 120
What is a Secured Credit Card 120
How Does FICO View A Secure Credit Card 121
Three Things That Matter In A Secure Credit Card 122
Secured Cards You Need 122
Non-Secured Cards Basics 124
Non-Secured Cards 126
Capital One QuicksilverOne Cash Rewards Credit Card 126
Credit One Bank Platinum Visa with Cash Back Rewards 126
Credit One Bank® Platinum Visa® for Rebuilding Credit 126
Fingerhut Credit Account issued by WebBank 126
Milestone® Gold Mastercard® 126
Credit One Bank® Unsecured Platinum Visa® 127
Avant Credit Card 127
Milestone® Mastercard® 127
Credit One Bank® NASCAR® Visa® Credit Card 127
Credit Card Holders 127
If You Have Credit Cards Don't Close Old Accounts 127
Don't Consolidate Debt Onto One Card 128
Important Things You Need To Know About Credit Card Debt 128
Decrease your Credit Utilization 129
Credit Utilization Components 130
The Amount Of Debt Still Owed Lenders 130
The Number Of Accounts With Debt Outstanding 130
The Amount Of Debt Owed On Individual Accounts 130
The Lack Of Certain Type Of Loans (Installment loans) 130
The Percentage Of Credit Line Use On Revolving Accounts 130
The Percentage Of Debt Still Owed On Installment Loans 130
Ace Your Credit Utilization 132
Things To Do For Best Credit Utilization 132
Pay Down Your Credit Cards 133
Increase Your Credit Limit 133
Apply for A New Credit Card 133
Get A Home Equity Line Of Credit 133
Buying A House 134
Personal Loan To Pay Off Credit Cards 134

My Experience: Finance Degree, 6 years loans officer at a national bank, 4 1/2 years credit bureau manager for one of the big three credit bureau's   John Harris

Get Added As An Authorized User	134
Pay To Be An Authorized User	136
Boostmyscore.net	136
Double All Your Cards	137
Deleting Items From Your Credit Report	137
www.dcrusa.com	138
Repairing Your Own Credit	140
3 Reasons You Never Dispute Things Online	140
Reason Number 1: Time	141
Reason Number 2: Shortcut The Process	141
Reason Number 3 : Revision Not In Your Favor "Verified"	141
Listen To The FTC	143
What The Credit Bureaus Should Do When They Get A Dispute	143
Here's What Really Happens When You Dispute	143
Your Credit Has Been Outsourced	144
E-Oscar Explained	144
E-Oscar Codes	145
Reasons of Dispute Percentages	146
Great News For You About Disputing	147
Because of the National Consumer Assistance Plan disputing items on your reports will be easier.	147
Reports Have Errors	148
Time To Dispute	149
Two Means of Disputes	149
The Secret to Disputing Accounts With The Credit Bureaus	149
Disputing with the Bureaus Must Do's	150
Dispute Addresses	151
GENERATION 1.0 LETTER	151
Identification Form GENERATION LETTER	152
Identification Form Requirements	153
Contacting the Bureau Requirements	154

Now Track Your letters	154
Possible Results	154
GENERATION 2.0 LETTER	155
Identification Form GENERATION LETTER	156
Identification Form Requirements	157
Contacting the Bureau Requirements	158
Now Track Your letters	158
GENERATION 3.0 LETTER	158
Identification Form GENERATION LETTER	159
Identification Form Requirements	160
Contacting the Bureau Requirements	161
Now Track Your letters	161
GENERATION 4.0 LETTER	162
Identification Form GENERATION LETTER	163
Identification Form Requirements	164
Contacting the Bureau Requirements	165
Now Track Your letters	165
GENERATION 5.0 LETTER	166
Identification Form GENERATION LETTER	167
Identification Form Requirements	168
Contacting the Bureau Requirements	169
Now Track Your letters	169
Small Claims Form Included	169
GENERATION 6.0 LETTER	170
Identification Form GENERATION LETTER	171
Identification Form Requirements	172
Contacting the Bureau Requirements	173
Now Track Your letters	173
Filling Your Complaint	173
Disputing With The Original Debtor	175
Steps to Dispute With Original Creditor	179
Letter to the Original Debtor	180
Identification Form	181
Identification Form Requirements	182
Contacting the Bureau Requirements	182
Now Track Your letters	182

My Experience: Finance Degree, 6 years loans officer at a national bank, 4 1/2 years credit bureau manager for one of the big three credit bureau's   John Harris

Last Option Pay For Deletion Letter 183
Final Note 184
www.dcrusa.com 184

Copyright © 2019 John Harris
All rights reserved.

LET'S GET STARTED

Ok, Let's start at the beginning. Recently you have probably found out your credit is not the greatest. It might not be your fault or it might not be, it doesn't really matter. You just want it fixed.

Many years ago I started working in the credit business. My first job was working as a loans officer for a national bank. My job was to get financing for people with very shaky credit.

Much of my pay was commission based. This really drove me to help people get the loans they needed. The only way to do this was to rapidly increase their credit score.

At first this seemed impossible but after a chance encounter with a man named Tom Bradley things started to change. Tom worked at a national credit bureau and we met at a business convention for the mortgage industry. Tom showed me many techniques on (TM)Rapid Rescoring and Quick Credit Repair Techniques. Well because of my success at funding these hard to get loans I was given a promotion to loans manager.

Me and Tom stayed in touch and a few years before he retired he got me a job at his credit bureau. When I first got there I was very surprised at how high up in the company he was. He took me under his wing and that's when school got kicked into high gear. Talk about a lesson on the credit industry. He showed me things that would be the difference between someone losing their house or not. It was very powerful stuff.

I could go on and on here about my experience working as a credit bureau manager or how I was a loans officer for 6 years but I won't bore you with all the details. This really is not about me anyways. It's about you and your credit. You can choose to believe me or not.

My Experience: Finance Degree, 6 years loans officer at a national bank, 4 1/2 years credit bureau manager for one of the big three credit bureau's   John Harris

THINGS I NEED YOU TO DO BEFORE WE START WITH THE REPAIR PROCESS

Ok look I know you might find these things I tell you crazy but you just need to trust me on these things. Most of you have probably heard of the book "THE SECRET" or now the TV show. The Author Rhonda Byrne is a very good friend of mine. Now I don't know how much you know about how the subconscious mind works but here goes.

1) Every morning when you wake up read a list of all the things you are appreciative that you have. For example a place to live a spouse etc. Really feel the appreciation.
2) Write this exact sentence every morning "I am the person with Great Credit."
3) Every night before bed visualize yourself at a car dealership or anywhere you need credit. See yourself saying "I have great credit" Really feel the great feeling of say "I have great credit".
4) Repeat out loud "I have great credit". Always do this in the present tense. This works the best in front of a mirror. Use your rear view mirror in your car. Setup your phone to alert you every 5 minutes. Say it out loud. You are brain washing your subconscious to believe this is a fact. Your subconscious will use its amazing power to make this true.
5) Visualize yourself signing into your Credit Karma account (more about this later) and this is what you see (picture on next page). Stare at this picture and feel how great it feels to have this great credit. Really stare at the picture.

DO NOT SKIP ANY OF THESE STEPS

PS: Live like you have great credit. When you drive by a car dealership or a house for sale imagine talking to the sales person.

REMEMBER KEEP SAYING "I AM THE PERSON WITH GREAT CREDIT"

==Say "I am the person with great credit". Play pretend in your mind. Soon your reality will catch up to your imagination.==

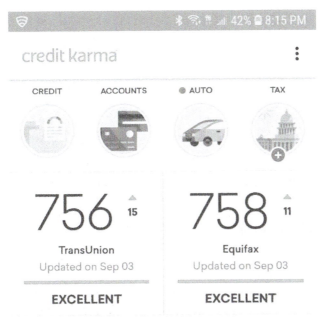

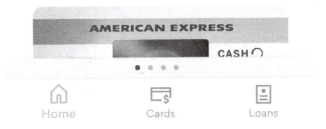

My Experience: Finance Degree, 6 years loans officer at a national bank, 4 1/2 years credit bureau manager for one of the big three credit bureau's   John Harris

WHAT IS CREDIT

Credit is borrowed money that you can use to purchase goods and services when you need them. You get credit from a credit grantor, whom you agree to pay back the amount you spent, plus applicable finance charges, at an agreed-upon time.
There are four types of credit:

Revolving Credit:
With revolving credit, you are given a maximum credit limit, and you can make charges up to that limit. Each month, you carry a balance (or revolve the debt) and make a payment. Most credit cards are a form of revolving credit.

Charge Cards:
While they often look like revolving credit cards and are used in the same way, charge accounts differ in that you must pay the total balance every month.

Service Credit:
Your agreements with service providers are all credit arrangements. You receive electricity, cellular phone service, gym membership, etc., with the agreement that you will pay for them each month. Not all service accounts are reported in your credit history.

Installment Credit:
With installment credit, a creditor loans you a specific amount of money, and you agree to repay the money and interest in regular installments of a fixed amount over a set period of time. Car loans and mortgages are two examples of installment credit.

NOTE: Now I know not a lot of people enjoy history lessons but, I have included the history of credit. It is interesting how long this system has been going on but if you feel like skipping this section I don't blame you.

History of Credit

The idea of exchanging goods or services in return for a promise of future payment developed only after centuries of trade: money and credit were unknown in the earliest stages of human history. Nevertheless, as early as 1300 B.C., loans were made among the Babylonians and Assyrians on the security of mortgages and advance deposits. By 1000 B.C., the Babylonians had already devised a crude form of the bill of exchange, so a creditor merchant could direct the debtor merchant in a distant place to pay a third party to whom the first merchant was indebted. Installment sales of real estate were being made by the Egyptians in the time of the Pharaohs.

Traders in the Mediterranean area, including Phoenicia, Greece, Rome and Carthage, also used credit. The vast boundaries of the Roman Empire, at the beginning of the Christian era, encouraged widespread trading and a broader use of credit. In the disorganized period that marked the decline and fall of the Roman Empire, credit bills of exchange or promissory notes were widely used to reduce the dangers and difficulties of transferring money through unorganized trading areas.

During the Middle Ages, a period which spanned 1000 years from about 500 to 1500 A.D., credit bills were essential to the trading activities of the prosperous Italian city-states. Lending and borrowing, as well as buying and selling on credit, became widespread practices; the debtor-creditor relationship was found in all classes of society from peasants to nobles, even including the Pope and other high dignitaries of the Church. A common form of investment and credit, especially in Italy, was the "sea loan" whereby the capitalist advanced money to the merchant and thus

My Experience: Finance Degree, 6 years loans officer at a national bank, 4 1/2 years credit bureau manager for one of the big three credit bureau's   John Harris

shared the risk. If the voyage was a success, the creditor got the investment back plus a substantial bonus of 20 to 30 percent; if the ship was lost, the creditor could lose the entire sum.

Another form of credit was the "fair letter" which was developed at the fairs held regularly in the centers of trading areas during the Middle Ages. The fair letter amounted to a promissory note to be paid before the end of the fair or at the time of the next fair. It enabled a merchant, who was short of cash, to secure goods on credit. This gave the merchant time either to sell the goods brought to the fair or to take home and sell the goods that had been purchased on credit.

Credit in Early America

The discovery of the New World provided new opportunities for the growth of capitalism and the expansion of credit. The first recorded use of open credit in early America took place with the establishment of the first permanent colony in New England. In September 1620, the Mayflower set sail from England for Virginia. Because of bad weather and navigational errors, the Pilgrims ended up off the coast of Cape Cod and eventually established the village of Plymouth in Massachusetts. While the journey itself was a tremendous achievement, so was its financing.

The Pilgrims had spent three years of arduous negotiations in England attempting to raise the funds necessary for the trip. A wealthy London merchant financed the trip and provided for "all credit advanced and to be advanced." In return, the Pilgrims contracted to work for a period of seven years. At the end of that period, payment would be made to the creditors based on the size of the individual investment.

The original credit of £1,800 could not be paid at the end of seven years, so an alternative arrangement was agreed upon: £200 to be paid annually for a term of nine years. This arrangement had to be renegotiated and finally, after 25 years, the last payment was made. This was the first example of credit in early America.

To finance the American Revolution, the Second Continental Congress made efforts to finance the Army of the United Colonies. The Congress had only three alternatives: borrow the money from sympathetic countries abroad which was an impossible task since the Colonist's credit in the world stood at zero; impose taxes which was unpopular and the very cause that had brought about the American Revolution; or issue bills of credit.

In June of 1775, the Continental Congress authorized the printing of $2,000,000 in various denominations ranging from one dollar to eight dollars. Trouble for the Continental currency began almost at once; each note had to be hand signed which was not a simple task considering 49,000 of them had to be signed. Counterfeiting of the currency was rampant. The principle behind the Continental currency was, in essence, a promise to pay the final bearer, at some point in the future, the face value in Spanish coins, the coins in widest circulation at this time.

In 1783, the Treaty of Paris was signed bringing an official end to the war and official recognition of the United States by England. Trading resumed and American importers and wholesalers extended generous terms to their customers. Generally, sales were made on terms of 12 months but even where six- or nine-month terms where offered, it was not uncommon for an account to remain unpaid for a much longer period, up to 24 months or more.

With the restoration of pre-Revolutionary trade customs and habits, credit references assumed importance, although in most instances, proper information was still lacking. Some prospective purchasers took the precaution of using the names of prominent people they knew when placing orders on credit. Credit references accompanied orders, however in most cases, merchants took their chances.

Terms of sale, as they developed during the 1800s, reflected the changes in the rapidly expanding economy. The 12-month period, which had prevailed, showed a tendency to become shorter. By the 1830s, the average term of sale was about six months.

Hard financial times hit the country in the mid 1830's. The population was rapidly growing and business was expanding. The sale of land on credit went virtually unchecked. The banking system was not centralized. By the summer of 1837, bank after bank closed its doors and thousands of businesses went into bankruptcy. The financial panic of 1837 saw the beginnings of the Mercantile Agency, established in 1841 by Lewis

My Experience: Finance Degree, 6 years loans officer at a national bank, 4 1/2 years credit bureau manager for one of the big three credit bureau's   John Harris

Tappan. It was this credit information agency which eventually became Dun & Bradstreet and helped transform credit, and with it, the course of American commerce.

The story of American credit, as we now know it, was not solely influenced by Dun & Bradstreet. Another organization important for credit managers worldwide was formed in 1896 in Toledo, Ohio. A group of credit executives, representing a hundred or so of their colleagues, organized themselves into a national association for credit managers, the National Association of Credit Men. Their exchange of credit information was initially conducted on a local and regional level. The association expanded into the National Association of Credit Management (NACM), which today with its network of Affiliated Associations, represents approximately 30,000 credit executives worldwide.

HISTORY OF CREDIT CARDS

NOTE: Here is where things get crazy. People start walking around with credit cards. You can spend money you don't have. Credit cards are a huge reason people have credit problems. They are here to stay so we are going to use them to our advantage.

As far back as the late 1800s, consumers and merchants exchanged goods through the concept of credit, using credit coins and charge plates as currency. It wasn't until about half a century ago that plastic payments as we know them today became a way of life.

Early beginnings
In the early 1900s, oil companies and department stories issued their own proprietary cards, according to Stan Sienkiewicz, in a paper for the Philadelphia Federal Reserve entitled "Credit Cards and Payment Efficiency." Such cards were accepted only at the business that issued the card and in limited locations. While modern credit cards are mainly used for convenience, these predecessor cards were developed as a means of creating customer loyalty and improving customer service.

The first bank card, named "Charge-It," was introduced in 1946 by John Biggins, a banker in Brooklyn, according to MasterCard. When a customer used it for a purchase, the bill was forwarded to Biggins' bank. The bank reimbursed the merchant and obtained payment from the customer.

The catches: Purchases could only be made locally, and Charge-It cardholders had to have an account at Biggins' bank.

In 1951, the first bank credit card appeared in New York's Franklin National Bank for loan customers. It also could be used only by the bank's account holders.

The Diners Club Card was the next step in credit cards, the story began in 1949 when a man named Frank McNamara had a business dinner in New York's Major's Cabin Grill.

When the bill arrived, Frank realized he'd forgotten his wallet. He managed to find his way out of the pickle, but he decided there should be an alternative to cash. McNamara and his partner, Ralph Schneider, returned to Major's Cabin Grill in February of 1950 and paid the bill with a small, cardboard card. Coined the Diners Club Card and used mainly for travel and entertainment purposes, it claims the title of the first credit card in widespread use.

Plastic debuts

By 1951, there were 20,000 Diners Club cardholders. A decade later, the card was replaced with plastic. Diners Club Card purchases were made on credit, but it was technically a charge card, meaning the bill had to be paid in full at the end of each month.

American Express formed in 1850. It specialized in deliveries as a competitor to the U.S. Postal Service, money orders (1882) and traveler's checks, which the company invented in 1891. The company discussed creating a travel charge card as early as 1946, but it was the launch of the rival Diners Club card that put things in motion.

In 1958 the company emerged into the credit card industry with its own product, a purple charge card for travel and entertainment expenses.

In 1959, American Express introduced the first card made of plastic (previous cards were made of cardboard or celluloid).

My Experience: Finance Degree, 6 years loans officer at a national bank, 4 1/2 years credit bureau manager for one of the big three credit bureau's   John Harris

American Express soon introduced local currency credit cards in other countries. About 1 million cards were being used at about 85,000 establishments within the first five years, both in and out of the U.S. In the 1990s, the company expanded into an all-purpose card. American Express, or Amex as it often is called, is about to celebrate its 50th credit card anniversary.

Closed-loop System

The Diners Club and American Express cards "functioned in what is known as a 'closed-loop' system, made up of the consumer, the merchant and the issuer of the card," Sienkiewicz writes. "In this structure, the issuer both authorizes and handles all aspects of the transaction and settles directly with both the consumer and the merchant."
In 1959, the option of maintaining a revolving balance was introduced, according to MasterCard. This meant cardholders no longer had to pay off their full bills at the end of each cycle. While this carried the risk of accumulating finance charges, it gave customers greater flexibility in managing their money.

Bank Card Associations

"The general-purpose credit card was born in 1966, when the Bank of America established the BankAmerica Service Corporation that franchised the BankAmericard brand (later to be known as Visa) to banks nationwide.
In 1966, a national credit card system was formed when a group of credit-issuing banks joined together and created the InterBank Card Association.

The ICA is now known as MasterCard Worldwide, though it was temporarily known as MasterCharge. This organization competes directly with a similar Visa program.

The new bank card associations were different from their predecessors in that an 'open-loop' system was now created, requiring interbank cooperation and funds transfers.

Visa and MasterCard's organizations both issue credit cards through member banks and set and maintain the rules for processing. They are both run by board members who are mostly high-level executives from their member banking organizations.

As the bank card industry grew, banks interested in issuing cards became members of either the Visa association or MasterCard association. Their members shared card program costs, making the bank card program available to even small financial institutions. Later, changes to the association bylaws allowed banks to belong to both associations and issue both types of cards to their customers.

Credit Card Processing Evolves

As credit card processing became more complicated, outside service companies began to sell processing services to Visa and MasterCard association members. This reduced the cost of programs for banks to issue cards, pay merchants and settle accounts with cardholders, thus allowing greater expansion of the payments industry.

Visa and MasterCard developed rules and standardized procedures for handling the bank card paper flow in order to reduce fraud and misuse of cards. The two associations also created international processing systems to handle the exchange of money and information and established an arbitration procedure to settle disputes between members.

Other Issuers Join the Party

Although American Express was among the first companies to issue a charge card, it wasn't until 1987 that it issued a credit card allowing customers to pay overtime rather than at the end of every month. Its original business model focused on the travel and entertainment charges made by business people, which involved significant revenue from merchants and annual membership fees from customers. While these products are still in its tool chest, the company has developed numerous no-annual fee credit cards offering low introductory rates and reward programs, similar to as traditional bank cards.

My Experience: Finance Degree, 6 years loans officer at a national bank, 4 1/2 years credit bureau manager for one of the big three credit bureau's   John Harris

Another relatively recent entry into the card business is Discover Card, originally part of the Sears Corporation. According to Discover, its first card was unveiled at the 1986 Super Bowl. Discover Card Services sought to create a new brand with its own merchant network, and the company has been successful at developing merchant acceptance.

A 2004 antitrust court ruling against Visa and MasterCard -- initiated by the U.S. government and the Department of Justice -- changed the exclusive relationship that Visa and MasterCard enjoyed with banks. It allows banks and other card issuers to provide customers with American Express or Discover cards, in addition to a Visa or MasterCard.

Whew, the history lesson is over. Now we need to get serious. First we need to know who we are dealing with here.

The Main Axis Players

Yes they are the AXIS and you should treat them like they are the enemy. We need to beat them at their own game. This is a game but with serious consequences as you probably already know.

There are three players on the axis side (we are going to make them allies by the end of this publication).

The Credit Bureaus also known as Credit Reporting Agencies (CRA's), Data Furnishers and FICO.

NOTE: So let's make it really simple to understand. Each has its own function to perform.

Data Furnishers provide the credit information.
Credit Reporting Agencies record the data.
FICO uses the information to generate a FICO score.

Here is a really simple example: Bank of America (Data Furnisher) has issued a credit card to John Doe. They send the information (like credit limit and amount owed etc.) to all the Credit Bureaus (TransUnion, Equifax, Experian) who record all the data.

John Doe wants another credit card from Chase Bank. So Chase Bank checks his credit through the bureaus to get a FICO score to see if he qualifies.

First Let's Look at Credit Reporting Agencies (CRA's)

Here is the definition of a Credit Bureau

cred·it bu·reau
/ˈkredət ˈbyo͝orō/
noun
    a company that collects information relating to the credit ratings of individuals and makes it available to credit card companies, financial institutions, etc.

There Are Three Credit Reporting Agencies (CRA's)

TransUnion, Equifax and Experian

NOTE: If you have trouble remembering them think of a Golf "TEE" The First Letter of Each Bureau "TEE". Here's the basics of each Credit Bureau.

My Experience: Finance Degree, 6 years loans officer at a national bank, 4 1/2 years credit bureau manager for one of the big three credit bureau's   John Harris

TransUnion®
EQUIFAX
⁙ Experian

Equifax, based in Atlanta, has 7,000 employees and "operations in the U.S. and 18 other countries including Argentina, Brazil, Canada, Chile, Costa Rica, Ecuador, El Salvador, Honduras, India, Ireland, Mexico, Paraguay, Peru, Portugal, Russia, Spain, the United Kingdom and Uruguay." Especially dominant in the southern and eastern sections of the U.S., it claims to be the market leader in most of the countries in which it has a presence.

Experian, whose domestic headquarters is in Costa Mesa, Calif., originally handled reports for the western United States. Now it promotes itself as "the leading global information services company." The firm "employs approximately 16,000 people in 39 countries and has its corporate headquarters in Dublin, Ireland, with operational headquarters in Nottingham, UK and São Paulo, Brazil."

TransUnion markets itself as a "global leader in credit information and information management services." The Chicago-based firm has "operations and affiliates in 33 countries." It employs approximately 3,700 people.

NOTE: Now I am going to give you some in depth information on these three Credit Bureaus. Do you really need to know this stuff? No not at all and if you want to skip these pages I don't blame you.

The reason I have included this information is some readers like to really get in depth with this kind of stuff. If that's not you just skip this section.

TransUnion Equifax and Experian In Depth

Experian In Depth

Experian is a global information services group with operations in 40 countries, with corporate headquarters in Dublin, Republic of Ireland and operational headquarters in Nottingham, United Kingdom; Costa Mesa, California, United States; São Paulo, Brazil; and Heredia, Costa Rica.

The company now employs 17,000 people. It is listed on the London Stock Exchange and is a constituent of the FTSE 100 Index. Experian is a partner in the UK government's Verify ID system.

In the UK during the 1970s, GUS plc, a retail conglomerate with millions of customers paying for goods on credit, employed John Peace, a computer programmer at the time, to combine the mail order data from various GUS businesses and create a central database to which was later added electoral roll data as well as county court judgements. GUS's database was commercialized in 1980 under the name Commercial Credit Nottingham (CCN). In 1996 GUS plc acquired the US credit reporting business Experian, formerly known as TRW Information Services, from Bain Capital and the Thomas H. Lee Partners and merged it into CCN.

During the next ten years, Experian broadened its product range to new industry sectors, beyond financial services, and entered new markets such as Latin America, Asia Pacific and Eastern Europe. The business expanded through both organic development and acquisitions. In October 2006 Experian was demerged from the British company GUS plc and listed on the London Stock Exchange.

In August 2005, Experian accepted a settlement with the Federal Trade Commission (FTC) over charges that Experian had violated a previous settlement with the FTC. The FTC's allegations concerned customers who signed up for the "free credit report" at Experian's Consumerinfo.com site. The FTC alleged that ads for the "free credit report" did not adequately disclose that Experian would automatically

My Experience: Finance Degree, 6 years loans officer at a national bank, 4 1/2 years credit bureau manager for one of the big three credit bureau's   John Harris

enroll customers in Experian's $79.95 credit-monitoring program.

In January 2008, Experian announced that it would cut more than 200 jobs at its Nottingham office as it moved development work to India to reduce costs.

Experian shut down its Canadian operations on 14 April 2009.

Experian's principal lines of business are credit services, marketing services, decision analytics and consumer services. The company collects information on people, businesses, motor vehicles and insurance. It also collects 'lifestyle' data from on- and off-line surveys.

Experian provides services in North America, Latin America, UK and Ireland, Europe, Middle East and Africa and Asia Pacific and reports its financial performance across those regions. Activities in these regions are grouped into four principal activities: credit services, decision analytics, marketing services and consumer services.

Like the other major credit reporting bureaus, Experian is chiefly regulated in the United States by the Fair Credit Reporting Act (FCRA). The Fair and Accurate Credit Transactions Act of 2003, signed into law in 2003, amended the FCRA to require the credit reporting companies to provide consumers with one free copy of their credit report per 12-month period. Like its main competitors, TransUnion and Equifax, Experian markets credit reports directly to consumers. Experian heavily markets its for-profit credit reporting service, FreeCreditReport.com, and all three agencies have been criticized and even sued for selling credit reports that can be obtained at no cost.

Experian refuses to follow California law with respect to disputes and relies only on the Fair Credit Reporting Act.

The company's largest operation is Experian North America, a consumer credit reporting agency that is considered one of the three largest American credit agencies along with Equifax and TransUnion.

Equifax In Depth

Equifax Inc. is a consumer credit reporting agency in the United States, considered one of the three largest American credit agencies along with Experian and TransUnion. Founded in 1899, Equifax is the oldest of the three agencies and gathers and maintains information on over 400 million credit holders worldwide.

Based in Atlanta, Georgia, Equifax is a global service provider with US $2.3 billion in annual revenue and 7,000+ employees in 14 countries. Equifax is listed on the NYSE.

Equifax was founded in Atlanta, GA, as Retail Credit Company in 1899. The company grew quickly and by 1920 had offices throughout the US and Canada. By the 1960s, Retail Credit Company was one of the nation's largest credit bureaus, holding files on millions of American and Canadian citizens.

Even though they still did credit reporting the majority of their business was making reports to insurance companies when people applied for new insurance policies including life, auto, fire and medical insurance. All of the major insurance companies used RCC to get information on health, habits, morals, use of vehicles and finances.

They also investigated insurance claims and made employment reports when people were seeking new jobs. Most of the credit work was then being done by a subsidiary, Retailers Commercial Agency.

Retail Credit Company's extensive information holdings, and its willingness to sell them to anyone, attracted criticism of the company in the 1960s and 1970s. These included that it collected "...facts, statistics, inaccuracies and rumors... about virtually every phase of a person's life; his marital troubles, jobs, school history, childhood, sex life, and political activities." The company was also alleged to reward its employees for collecting negative information on consumers.

As a result, when the company moved to computerize its records, which would lead to much wider availability of the personal information it held, the US Congress held hearings in 1970.

These led to the enactment of the Fair Credit Reporting Act in the same year which gave consumers rights regarding information stored about them in corporate databanks. It is alleged that the hearings prompted the Retail Credit Company to change its name to Equifax in 1975 to improve

My Experience: Finance Degree, 6 years loans officer at a national bank, 4 1/2 years credit bureau manager for one of the big three credit bureau's   John Harris

its image.

The company later expanded into commercial credit reports on companies in the US, Canada and the UK, where it came into competition with companies such as Dun & Bradstreet and Experian. The insurance reporting was phased out. The company also had a division selling specialist credit information to the insurance industry but spun off this service, including the Comprehensive Loss Underwriting Exchange (CLUE) database as ChoicePoint in 1997. The company formerly offered digital certification services, which it sold to GeoTrust in September 2001.

In the same year, Equifax spun off its payment services division, forming the publicly listed company Certegy, which subsequently acquired Fidelity National Information Services in 2006. Certegy effectively became a subsidiary of Fidelity National Financial as a result of this reverse acquisition merger.

For most of its existence, Equifax has operated primarily in the business-to-business sector, selling consumer credit and insurance reports and related analytics to businesses in a range of industries. Business customers include retailers, insurance firms, healthcare providers, utilities, government agencies, as well as banks, credit unions, personal and specialty finance companies and other financial institutions.
Equifax sells businesses credit reports, analytics, demographic data, and software. Credit reports provide detailed information on the personal credit and payment history of individuals, indicating how they have honored financial obligations such as paying bills or repaying a loan. Credit grantors use this information to decide what sort of products or services to offer their customers, and on what terms.

Equifax also provides commercial credit reports, similar to Dun & Bradstreet, containing financial and non-financial data on businesses of all sizes. Equifax collects and provides data through the NCTUE, an exchange of non-credit data including consumer payment history on telco and utility accounts.

From 1999, Equifax began offering services to the credit consumer sector in addition, such as credit fraud and identity theft prevention products. Equifax, and other credit monitoring agencies are required by law to provide US residents with one free credit file disclosure every 12 months; the Annualcreditreport website incorporates data from US Equifax credit records.

TransUnion In Depth

TransUnion is an American company that provides credit information and information management services to approximately 45,000 businesses and approximately 500 million consumers worldwide in 33 countries. It is also the third-largest credit bureau in the United States.

Like major competitors Equifax and Experian, TransUnion markets credit reports directly to consumers. The company is based in Chicago, Illinois, and its revenue in 2014 was US$1.3 billion.

TransUnion was originally formed in 1968 as a holding company for the railroad leasing organization, Union Tank Car Company. The following year, it acquired the Credit Bureau of Cook County, which possessed and maintained 3.6 million card files. In 1981, a Chicago-based holding company The Marmon Group acquired TransUnion for approximately $688 million.

Almost thirty years later, in 2010, Goldman Sachs Capital Partners and Advent International acquired it from Madison Dearborn Partners In 2014, TransUnion acquired Hank Asher's data company TLO. On June 25, 2015, TransUnion became a publicly traded company for the first time, trading under the symbol TRU.

TransUnion has evolved its business over the years to offer products and services for both businesses and consumers. For businesses, TransUnion has evolved its traditional credit score offering to include trended data that helps predict consumer repayment and debt behavior. This product, referred to as CreditVision, launched in Oct. 2013.

Its SmartMove service facilitates credit and background checks for consumers who may be serving in a landlord capacity.

In September 2013, the company acquired eScan Data Systems of Austin to provide post-service eligibility determination support to hospitals and healthcare systems. The technology was integrated into TransUnion's ClearIQ platform that tracks patients demographic and insurance related information to support benefit verification.

In November 2013, TransUnion merged with TLO LLC, a company that

My Experience: Finance Degree, 6 years loans officer at a national bank, 4 1/2 years credit bureau manager for one of the big three credit bureau's   John Harris

leverages data in support of its investigative and risk management tools. Its TLOxp technology aggregates data sets and using a proprietary algorithm to uncover relationships between data that were not possible before.

As part of its fraud protection products, it also offers business a tool called DecisionEdge that aggregates the data needed to prevent fraud through a system that customizes the information needed to finalize a transaction.

For consumers, TransUnion offers credit monitoring and identity theft protection tools. The company's app offers a function called CreditLock that allows an individual to unlock and lock their credit to help protect against fraudulent activity.

In 2003, Judy Thomas of Klamath Falls, Oregon, was awarded $5.3 million in a successful lawsuit against TransUnion. The award was made on the grounds that it took her six years to get TransUnion to remove incorrect information in her credit report.

In 2006, after spending two years trying to correct erroneous credit information that resulted from being a victim of identity theft, a fraud victim named Sloan filed suit against all three of the USA's largest credit agencies. TransUnion and Experian settled out of court for an undisclosed amount. In Sloan v. Equifax, a jury awarded Sloan $351,000. She wrote letters. She called them. They saw the problem. They just didn't fix it.

TransUnion has also been criticized for concealing charges. Many users complained of not being aware of a $17.95/month charge for holding a TransUnion account.

In March 2015, following a settlement with the New York Attorney General, TransUnion, along with other credit reporting companies, Experian and Equifax, agreed to help consumers with errors and red flags on credit reports. Under the new settlement, credit-reporting firms are required to use trained employees to respond when a consumer flags a mistake on their file.

These employees are responsible for communicating with the lender and resolving the dispute.

Things You Should Know About The Credit Bureaus

All the Credit Reporting Agencies Have Different Reports On You

All of these companies have different reports on you. This is because they don't share information about you with each other. They are competitors with each other. Each wants their own information, it's how they make money.

Suppose you apply for a loan, line of credit or credit card from a lender. That lender almost certainly performs a credit check, requesting that a report on you be run, from at least one of the three major credit bureaus. But it does not have to use all three. The lender might have a preferred relationship or value one credit scoring or reporting system over the other two.

All credit inquiries are noted in your credit report, but they only show up for the bureaus whose reports are pulled. If a credit inquiry is only sent to Experian, then Equifax and TransUnion do not know about it, for example.

Similarly, not all lenders report credit activity to each credit bureau. So a credit report from one company can differ from another. Lenders that do report to all three agencies may see their data appear on credit reports at different times simply because each bureau compiles data at different times of the month. Delinquency generally doesn't affect your credit score until at least 45 days have passed.

Credit Reporting Agencies Are NOT Government Agencies

Note: This amazes me to this day I travel the country speaking at Universities and Corporations on Credit Repair. Many attendees still ask my questions pertaining to Credit Bureaus being Government Agencies.

Although credit bureaus are **private companies**, they are highly

My Experience: Finance Degree, 6 years loans officer at a national bank, 4 1/2 years credit bureau manager for one of the big three credit bureau's   John Harris

regulated under the Fair Credit Reporting Act, or FCRA (More about this later). They are limited in how they collect, disburse and disclose consumer information, and have come under increased scrutiny since the Great Recession of 2007.

How do Credit Reporting Agencies Make Money

Note: That's a great question. They need to make money right? Well they do make money and lots of it. One interesting feature about the
credit bureau business model is how information is exchanged. Banks, financing companies, retailers and landlords send consumer credit information to the credit bureaus for free, and then the credit bureaus turn around and sell consumer information right back to them. Here is how it all works on a financial perspective.

All three Credit Bureaus obtain and sell information in similar ways.

On the surface, the financial arrangement between lenders and credit bureaus does not make much sense: Credit granters provide consumer credit information to bureaus for free, then they pay to have credit information sent back to them. The credit bureaus are able to collect, aggregate, synthesize and analyze the enormous quantity of information sent to them.

Four Data Products Sold by Credit Bureaus

All Credit Bureaus sell four data products: credit services, decision analytics, marketing and consumer assistance services.

Credit Services: Credit services are what most people think of when it comes to credit bureaus. The credit bureau receives a request from a lender for a consumer credit report, which the bureau sells to the lender.

Decision Analytics: Credit bureaus do not just want to sell a history of borrower payments. Instead, the bureaus package detailed transaction history with analytics about the way an individual interacts with certain debt. Lenders pay more for these reports.

Marketing: While it is not a traditional form of marketing, lenders that offer pre-approved credit are paying a marketing fee to a credit bureau for a list of consumers who meet predetermined requirements.

Consumer Services: Credit bureaus also interact directly with consumers, usually through credit monitoring, identity theft protection and fraud prevention. These services have become increasingly popular as the risk of identity theft has grown.

The Data Furnishers

Where do the Credit Reporting Agencies Get the information

My Experience: Finance Degree, 6 years loans officer at a national bank, 4 1/2 years credit bureau manager for one of the big three credit bureau's   John Harris

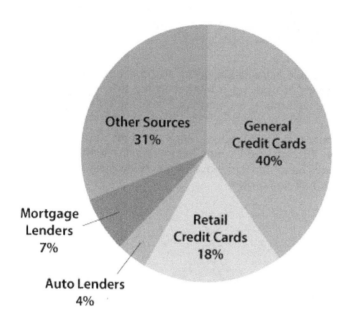

In the U.S., consumer reporting agencies collect and aggregate personal information, financial data, and alternative data on individuals from a variety of sources called data furnishers (such as banks, credit unions, consumer credit card companies, retailers, and auto finance companies and the courts i.e. public records) with which the reporting agencies have a relationship.

The data provided by the furnishers as well as collected by the bureaus are then aggregated into the consumer reporting agency's data repository or files. The resulting information is made available on request to customers of the consumer reporting agencies' for the purposes of credit risk assessment, credit scoring or for other purposes such as employment consideration or leasing an apartment.

Data furnishers that report consumer credit account data on a regular basis to credit reporting agencies, have duties under the Fair Credit Reporting Act (FCRA) to correct and update that consumer credit history information.

To assist data furnishers (such as banks, credit unions, consumer credit card companies, retailers, and auto finance companies) in this process, the credit reporting industry has adopted a standard electronic data reporting format called the Metro 2® Format.

Data Furnishers Are Required By The FCRA Fair Credit Reporting Act (More About This Later) to Comply With These Regulations

Now again this might be a lot of regulations you might want to just breeze over. It's not necessary to know every regulation that Data Furnishers are required to comply with. They have been included for those readers that want to know everything. So here goes and for those readers who are not interested jump to the section "FICO"

Guidelines for Data Furnishers Policies and Procedures from FCRC

You must establish and implement written policies and procedures regarding the accuracy and integrity of information you furnish to a CRA.

Your policies and procedures: must be appropriate to the nature, size, complexity, and scope of your activities; must be reviewed periodically and updated, as necessary; should ensure that information provided to a CRA is for the right person, and reflects the terms of the account and the consumer's performance on the account;

require maintenance of records for a reasonable amount of time;

establish internal controls for the accuracy and integrity of information, such as through random sampling; prevent re-aging (inaccurately changing the date of first delinquency on a consumer's account to a later date) and duplicative reporting, particularly following portfolio acquisitions or sales, mergers, and other transfers; and require updating of furnished information where necessary. Information should: be substantiated by your records when it is furnished; include consumer identifiers, like name(s), date of birth, Social Security number, telephone number(s), or

My Experience: Finance Degree, 6 years loans officer at a national bank, 4 1/2 years credit bureau manager for one of the big three credit bureau's   John Harris

address(es); and be furnished in a standardized form and specify the time period it pertains to.

Correct and Update Information

If you furnish information to a CRA on a regular basis and determine that any information you provided is inaccurate or incomplete, you must promptly notify the CRA and provide corrections or additions. Going forward, you must furnish only the correct information to the CRA. FCRA 623(a)(2)(B)

Furnishing Specific Items

The FCRA requires that if you furnish any information to a CRA, you must include any of the following items that are applicable to you.

Credit Limits — Usually, you must include a consumer's credit limit.

Disputed Information — Once a consumer disputes information, you may not report that information to a CRA without telling the CRA

Closed Accounts — If you furnish information to a CRA on a regular basis, you must notify the CRA that a consumer has voluntarily closed an account the next time you send information that would normally include that account. This is important because some users of information may interpret a closed account as an indicator of bad credit unless you clearly disclose that the consumer, not the creditor, closed the account. FCRA 623(a)(4)

Delinquent Accounts — When you refer an account for collection and notify a CRA that you have done so, you also must report the date of delinquency to the CRA within 90 days. The date of delinquency is the month and year the consumer's delinquency resulting in the referral began, see the examples below. FCRA 623(a)(5)(A)

If you are a debt collector furnishing information to a CRA about the accounts of a creditor, you must report the date of delinquency given to you by the creditor. FCRA 623(a)(5)(A) This "date of delinquency" determines how long the debt can be reported on a consumer's credit report. Generally, a CRA may report a delinquent debt for seven years from the date of delinquency. If the debt was discharged in bankruptcy, however, a CRA may report it for 10 years.

If the creditor didn't report the date of delinquency, you have two options:

You may establish and follow reasonable procedures to determine the date from the original creditor or another reliable source, or If you can't determine the date, you may establish and follow reasonable procedures to ensure that the reported date of delinquency is a date **before** the account was referred to collection or charged off. FCRA 623(a)(5)(B)

Negative Information from Financial Institutions — If you are a financial institution (as defined in the Gramm-Leach-Bliley Act) that extends credit and regularly reports A negative information about your customers to a nationwide CRA (for example, Equifax, Experian, or TransUnion), you must notify your customers that you report such negative information. Examples of negative information include a customer's delinquencies, late payments, insolvency, or any form of default. FCRA 623(a)(7)(G)(i)

You must provide the notice either before you furnish the negative information or within 30 days of furnishing it. You may include the notice with a notice of default, a billing statement, or another item sent to the consumer, but you **cannot** send it with a Truth In Lending Act notification. The notices must be clear and conspicuous.

The Consumer Financial Protection Bureau has model disclosures at 12 CFR Part 1022, Appendix B, FCRA 623(a)(7).

Medical Information — If your primary business is providing medical services, products, or devices, and you, your agent, or your assignee reports information about consumers to CRAs, you must notify each CRA that you are a medical provider. FCRA 623(a)(9) This notice helps the CRAs comply with their FCRA duties with regard to the reporting of medical information. FCRA 604(g) For example, if the name, address, and telephone number of a medical information furnisher appears on a consumer report, the information must be encoded so it doesn't identify the specific provider or the nature of the services, products, or devices. FCRA 605(a)(6)(A)

My Experience: Finance Degree, 6 years loans officer at a national bank, 4 1/2 years credit bureau manager for one of the big three credit bureau's   John Harris

The federal banking agencies have issued rules to implement these requirements.

DISPUTES

Consumers may dispute information that you furnished in two ways:

They may submit a dispute to the CRA.

They may submit a dispute directly to you.

Disputes to CRAs

If a CRA notifies you that a consumer disputes information you provided, you must:

investigate the dispute and review all relevant information provided by the CRA about the dispute; report your findings to the CRA;

provide corrected information to every CRA that received the information if your investigation shows the information is incomplete or inaccurate; and modify the information, delete it, or permanently block its reporting if the information turns out to be inaccurate or incomplete or can't be verified. FCRA 623(b)(1)

You must complete these steps within the same time allowed under the FCRA for the CRA to resolve the dispute. Normally, this is 30 days after the CRA gets the dispute from the consumer. If the consumer provides additional relevant information during the 30-day period, the CRA has 15 more days to resolve the dispute. The CRA must give you all the relevant information it gets within five business days of receipt, and must promptly give you additional relevant information provided by the consumer. If you don't investigate and respond to the notification of the dispute within the specified times, the CRA must delete the disputed information from its files. FCRA 623(b)(2) and 611(a)(1)

Disputes to Furnishers

You must investigate a consumer's dispute if it relates to:

the consumer's liability for a credit account or other debt with you. For example, disputes relating to whether there is or has been identity theft or fraud against the consumer, whether there is individual or joint liability on an account, or whether the consumer is an authorized user of a credit account;

the terms of a credit account or other debt with you. For example, disputes relating to the type of account, principal balance, scheduled payment amount on an account, or the amount of the credit limit on an open-end account;

the consumer's performance or other conduct concerning an account or other relationship with you. For example, disputes relating to the current payment status, high balance, date a payment was made, amount of a payment made, or date an account was opened or closed; or

any other information in a consumer report about an account or relationship with you that affects the consumer's creditworthiness, credit standing, credit capacity, character, general reputation, personal characteristics, or lifestyle. Furnisher Rule 660.4(a)

You must:

conduct a reasonable investigation review all relevant information provided by the consumer report results to the consumer, generally within 30 days notify each CRA to which you provided inaccurate information if the investigation finds the information was inaccurate. Furnisher Rule 660.4(e)

You are **not** required to investigate the dispute if it relates to:

the consumer's identifying information on a consumer report, including name, date of birth, Social Security number, phone number, or address; the names of previous or current employers; inquiries or requests for consumer reports;

information from public records, including judgments, bankruptcies, and liens; information related to fraud alerts or active duty alerts;

information provided to a CRA by another furnisher; or when you believe that the dispute is submitted by, prepared on behalf of the consumer by, or submitted on a form supplied to the consumer by a credit repair organization. Furnisher Rule 660.4(b)

You also are **not** required to investigate disputes that are frivolous or irrelevant, as defined by the Rule: the consumer didn't provide enough information the dispute is substantially the same as a dispute previously submitted you already fulfilled your obligation, and there is no new information.

If a dispute is found to be frivolous or irrelevant, you must notify the consumer within five business days of receiving the dispute. This notice can be a form letter. Include the reason for the determination and, if

My Experience: Finance Degree, 6 years loans officer at a national bank, 4 1/2 years credit bureau manager for one of the big three credit bureau's   John Harris

relevant, any information the consumer needs to submit so you can investigate the disputed information.

ADDITIONAL RESPONSIBILITIES
Victims of Identity Theft

When you are notified by a CRA that a consumer's identity has been stolen, you have specific duties under the FCRA. FCRA 605B

If a CRA notifies you that information you furnished is being blocked on a consumer's credit report because of identity theft, you must have procedures to prevent the re-reporting of the information. FCRA 623(a)(6)(A)

If a CRA notifies you that a debt has resulted from identity theft, you may not sell, transfer, or place that debt for collection. FCRA 615(f)(1)

If a consumer notifies you that he is a victim of identity theft, and gives you an identity theft report, you may not furnish information to a CRA regarding the fraudulent account or debt. FCRA 623(a)(6)(B)

If you find that you furnished inaccurate information due to identity theft, you must promptly notify each CRA of the correct information. Going forward, you must report only complete and accurate information. FCRA 623(a)(2)

If you provide credit, goods, or services to consumers, you may be required to supply application or other transaction records to an identity theft victim or law enforcement officer, if they ask. FCRA 605B(f) 615(g)

If you establish or extend credit plans or accounts, you may be required to follow certain steps to verify a consumer's identity when you see a fraud or active duty alert on his credit report. FCRA 605A(h)(B)(ii)

Whew, Ok so the Data Furnishers have a lot of rules to follow. Now let's talk about the last Axis Player the FICO Score.

FICO

FICO is a software company based in San Jose, California and founded by Bill Fair and Earl Isaac in 1956. Its FICO score, a measure of consumer credit risk, has become a fixture of consumer lending in the United States The name FICO comes from the company's original name, the Fair Isaac Co. It was often shortened to FICO and finally became the company's official name several years ago.

To create credit scores, they use information provided by one of the three major credit reporting agencies — Equifax, Experian or TransUnion. **But FICO itself is not a credit reporting agency. ALWAYS REMEMBER THIS FACT.**

FICO, is a company that specializes in what's known as "***predictive analytics***," which means they take information and analyze it to predict what's likely to happen.

So basically FICO is an educated "Fortune Teller". There are millions of people that have done exactly like YOU in regards to credit. The FICO company has computed all the results and they give you a score.

The FICO system assigns you a three-digit number that indicates your ability to pay back loans. FICO scores range from 300 to 850, and the national average FICO score is 695.

Your credit score is akin to a school **GPA**. It's a number that measures your success to others, in this case grading you as a credit-worthy individual.

Why FICO?

Now you might ask me why lenders need FICO?

My Experience: Finance Degree, 6 years loans officer at a national bank, 4 1/2 years credit bureau manager for one of the big three credit bureau's   John Harris

The central reason lenders use FICO scores when making lending decisions and determining what interest rate you qualify for is to gauge the likelihood that you'll become delinquent or default on your obligations. Here is the exact break down.

Here's how the FICO scores break down as compared to a borrower becoming seriously delinquent:

- **Exceptional — 800 and above:** Only 1 percent of these borrowers are likely to become seriously delinquent.
- **Very good — 740 to 799:** About 2 percent of these consumers might become seriously delinquent.
- **Good — 670 to 739:** Approximately 8 percent of these borrowers might become seriously delinquent.
- **Fair — 580 to 669:** About 28 percent of people in this bracket will become seriously delinquent.
- **Poor — Below 580:** Around 61 percent of these borrowers will become seriously delinquent.

Note: So you can see if you are a lender you have a 8% chance of someone with GOOD credit going seriously delinquent but a 61% change of someone with POOR credit going delinquent. Lenders adjust interest rates to compensate for the extra risk. Who would you rather lend your money to someone with good credit or poor credit? It's obvious to you and lenders.

Now the FICO is the most widely used broad-based risk score and the FICO Score plays a critical role in billions of decisions each year. The latest US version, FICO Score 9 is the most current and predictive FICO Score.

How Does FICO Make Money?

Note: That's another great question. They need to make money right? Well they do make money and lots of it.

The FICO Score is a **proprietary** model created by Fair Isaac Corporation (FICO).

Proprietary is the key word here. Here is the definition of proprietary:

Definition of *proprietary*
One that possesses, owns, or holds exclusive right to something.

Think of FICO as a Microsoft. While Microsoft has a program (Windows) that runs your computer. FICO has software that generates a risk score for lenders.

FICO primarily makes money by licensing their credit scoring model to credit bureaus. The credit bureaus, in turn, sell FICO scores and credit reports with FICO scores to banks, lenders and bankcard issuers. Fair Issac Corporation also sells credit reports and FICO scores to consumers through their Get your FICO Score, Credit Reports, Identity Theft Detection & Lost Wallet Protection website.

How is your Credit Score (FICO) calculated

Due to the proprietary nature of the FICO score, the Fair Isaac company does not reveal the exact formula it uses to compute this number. However, what is known is that the calculation is broken into five major categories with varying levels of importance. These categories, with weight in brackets, are payment history (35%), amount owed (30%), length of credit history (15%), new credit (10%) and type of credit used (10%).

All of these categories are taken into account in your overall score - no one area or incident determines your score.

The payment history category reviews how well you have met your prior

My Experience: Finance Degree, 6 years loans officer at a national bank, 4 1/2 years credit bureau manager for one of the big three credit bureau's   John Harris

obligations on various account types.

It also looks for previous problems in your payment history such as bankruptcy, collections and delinquency. It takes into consideration the size of these problems, the time it took to resolve them, and how long it has been since the problems appeared. The more problems you have in your credit history, the weaker your credit score will be.

The next largest component is the amount that you currently owe to lenders. While this category focuses on your current amount of debt, it also looks at the number of different accounts and the specific types of accounts that you hold. This area is focused on your present financial situation, and a large amount of debt from many sources will have an adverse effect on your score.

The other categories (length of credit history, new credit and type of credit used) are fairly straightforward.

The longer you have a good credit history, the better. Common sense dictates that someone who has never been late with payment over twenty years is a much safer bet than someone who has been on time for two.

Also, people who apply for credit a lot probably already have financial pressures causing them to do so, so each time you apply for credit, your score gets dinged a little. And finally, a person with only one credit card is less risky than a person with 10, so the more types of credit accounts you have, the lower your score will be.

It is important to understand that your credit score only looks at the information contained on your credit report and does not reflect additional information that your lender may consider in its appraisal. For example, your credit report does not include such things as current income and length of employment.

Note: As we move on in this publication I am going to give you some numbers that FICO doesn't want you to know.

More FICO Scores

Note: FICO has gone through many changes throughout the years. Just like Microsoft Windows. There are different versions. There are also industry specific versions. Here is the breakdown.

PS: FICO9 is the most recent version but most lenders still use FICO8

Experian
Most widely used version: FICO 8
Versions used in auto lending:
FICO Auto Score 8 or FICO Auto Score 2
Versions used in credit card decisioning:
FICO Bankcard Score 8 or FICO Bankcard Score 2
Versions used in mortgage lending
FICO Score 2

Equifax
Most widely used version: FICO 8
Versions used in auto lending
FICO Auto Score 8 or FICO Auto Score 5
Versions used in credit card decisioning
FICO Bankcard Score 8 or FICO Bankcard Score 5
Versions used in mortgage lending
FICO® Score 5

TransUnion
Most widely used version: FICO 8
Versions used in auto lending
FICO Auto Score 8 or FICO Auto Score 4
Versions used in credit card decisioning
FICO Bankcard Score 8 or FICO Bankcard Score 4
Versions used in mortgage lending
FICO Score 4

Note: I know what you are thinking. Why all these FICO scores? This is one crazy situation. Well I agree and to be honest you will have 65 FICO scores once FICO 9 is fully implemented. Whew that's a lot of FICO scores.

Why All The Different FICOS?

My Experience: Finance Degree, 6 years loans officer at a national bank, 4 1/2 years credit bureau manager for one of the big three credit bureau's   John Harris

Industry-specific FICO Score versions are designed to predict the chances of not paying as agreed in the future on a specific type of credit obligation - such as an auto loan or a credit card. They provide a lender with a refined prediction of risk for that particular type of credit.

FICO 2, 4, and 5 are very similar. The main differences between the three is that 2, 4,and 5 use data from Experian, TransUnion, and Equifax respectively. Mortgage lenders pull one of each and compile the reports in a document called a Residential Mortgage Credit Report. Duplicate data is screened and removed, and the middle score of the three is picked to represent your worthiness to pay back the mortgage.

FICO 8 and 9 use data from a single credit bureau, so using FICO 2, 4, and 5 together gives mortgage lenders a more complete view of your creditworthiness because they can see the history of every account you've opened. This is especially helpful for mortgage lenders as many creditors don't report account history to all three credit bureaus.

Note: Take a deep breath it's not really that complicated, a credit card provider wants a score with a higher weight on how you have paid credit cards in the past. An auto lender wants more weight on how you have done with car payments in the past. FICO has created models to accommodate this need.

PS: Get a good FICO 8 score and you will be fine with the others. Later I will show you how to access all the versions.

Interesting FICO Score Information

Annual Income	Average Credit Score
$30,000 or less	590
$30,001 - $49,999	643
$50,000 - $74,999	737

PS: Even though income is not calculated into a FICO you can see a definite higher score average for higher income people.

Region	Average Credit Score
Northeast	676
South	657
Midwest	680
West	676

The Newest FICO Score....Drum Roll Please .....FICO 9

My Experience: Finance Degree, 6 years loans officer at a national bank, 4 1/2 years credit bureau manager for one of the big three credit bureau's   John Harris

Medical Collections

The big change is how FICO 9 treats unpaid medical bills. The FICO 9 formula treats medical bills sent to collections differently than other debts. These debts won't ding your credit as much as non-medical debts sent to collection. The change follows studies by the Consumer Finance Protection Bureau.

This change is sensible. Medical debt is often for things outside of our control. Consumers may overspend on vacations and electronics, but they are less likely to be addicted to emergency room visits.

FICO 9 differentiates unpaid medical accounts in collections from unpaid non-medical accounts in collections. FICO's research found that unpaid medical accounts were less indicative of credit risk than unpaid non-medical accounts. In fact, building the most predictive credit score requires treating medical collections this way.

Paid Collections

A second significant change with FICO 9 is the score's treatment of paid collections. When a debt is sent to collections, it understandably hurts a consumer's credit score. The new credit score formula, however, disregards any collection matters that the consumer has paid in full.

Rent Payments Will Count

A final big change deals with rent payments. Under FICO 9, rental payment history is factored into the score when a landlord reports the payments to a credit bureau. This change can be particularly helpful to those with a limited credit history.

Despite all the excitement surrounding FICO 9, it's not the most widely used FICO formula. That honor still belongs to the earlier version, FICO 8. Why?

There may be several reasons. First, it's expensive for a bank or lender to change their underwriting process. Financial institutions no doubt undertake substantial testing of any new scoring model, and this takes time and money. Second, they may be perfectly happy with FICO 8. As they say, if it ain't broke, don't fix it

Here are the things to remember

FICO itself is not a credit reporting agency.
FICO primarily makes money by licensing their credit scoring model to credit bureaus.
FICO is by far the most widely used broad-based risk score
FICO uses information provided by one of the major credit reporting agencies Equifax, Experian or TransUnion to create the FICO score.

Ok, take a deep breath there is another score and I promise this is almost the last one. It's called the VantageScore.

VantageScore

VantageScore is a credit scoring model that first emerged in 2006 as a joint venture of the big three credit bureaus — Experian, Equifax and TransUnion — and now has the distinction of being one of only two scoring models lenders rely on to make lending decisions (the other being FICO obviously). VantageScore currently claims about 10% of this hard-to-crack market for credit scores used in the lending industry, with the greatest adoption seen among the largest banks and lenders.

VantageScore 3.0, introduced in March 2013, is the most recent version of the scoring model. This version of their model not only provides scores to general consumers but also helps 30 to 35 million adults who may not have a credit profile with alternative models, whether because they're new to the world of credit or don't use credit frequently.

Like other credit scores, your Vantage credit score consists of calculations that rely entirely on credit bureau information not income, bank accounts or other assets to predict how likely you are

My Experience: Finance Degree, 6 years loans officer at a national bank, 4 1/2 years credit bureau manager for one of the big three credit bureau's   John Harris

to pay your credit obligations on time each month. Your scores are impacted by your habits of paying on time, keeping debt balances low in relation to your total credit limits, the age of your credit accounts, the variety of accounts you have and the number of inquiries on your credit reports.

New Advantages of VantageScore 3.0

Without a doubt, the most radical feature of VantageScore 3.0 is its ability to calculate a score for 30 to 35 million previously "un-scoreable," or "thin file," consumers. While many other scoring models require at least six months of credit history and recent credit report updates, this model only requires one month of credit history and less frequent updates. This makes it possible for those consumers to have easier access to credit.

Other notable improvements include:
Ignoring all paid collections, as well as any collections, paid or unpaid, under $250
A new score range of 300 to 850, the same scale used by FICO, making it easier for consumers to interpret and manage their credit scores.
Credit relief for disaster victims by ignoring accounts negatively impacted by natural disasters.

VantageScore vs FICO

VantageScore and FICO scores are different credit scores. FICO, the original creator of the FICO Score, was not involved with the creation of VantageScore's new formula.

The big three credit bureaus — Experian, Equifax and TransUnion have advertised the VantageScore as something that will help banks and lenders further drill down into the "subprime" categories. Subprime lenders are banks or other lenders dedicated to borrowers with less than perfect credit or harder to substantiate credit.

By creating the VantageScore the bureaus hope to one day eliminate FICO. This will probably never happen as FICO is so embedded in lenders systems.

FICO / VantageScore Differences

The FICO score bases its credit scoring formula on five categories of information, while the VantageScore uses six.

FICO Score

- 35% payment history
- 30% level of debt
- 15% age of credit history
- 10% types of credit
- 10% credit inquiries

VantageScore 3.0

- Payment history - 40%
- Age and type of credit - 21%
- Percent of credit used - 20%
- Total balances/debt - 11%
- Recent credit behavior and inquiries - 5%
- Available credit - 3%

VantageScore 2.0

- 32% payment history
- 23% utilization
- 15% balances
- 13% depth of credit
- 10% recent credit
- 7% available credit

Both the FICO and VantageScore credit scoring formulas give about the same amount of percentages for payment history and new credit

My Experience: Finance Degree, 6 years loans officer at a national bank, 4 1/2 years credit bureau manager for one of the big three credit bureau's   John Harris

inquiries. But, there's a big difference in the treatment of utilization, age of credit history, and types of credit.

FICO gives utilization 30% of its credit score, while the VantageScore places a heavy 45% on how much credit you're using.

FICO gives a total 25% to age of credit history and types of credit. The VantageScore gives these two factors 13%.

Note: Whew just when you thought 65 FICO scores was enough we add the VantageScore. Now here's some scores that just need a quick mention and I promised no more scores.

Other Credit Scores

The non-FICO scores are called FAKO scores by some consumers. Experian has a credit score for educational use only (Plus Score) between 330 and 830, and Experian Scorex PLUS score is between 300 and 900. Equifax has the Equifax Credit Score between 280 and 850.

Some lenders use an Application Score between 100 and 990, and Credit Optics Score by ID Analytics Inc. between 1 and 999.

TransUnion's TransRisk New Account Score in the website Credit Karma is between 300 and 850, and Experian National Equivalency Score in Credit Sesame and Credit.com ranges from 360 to 840.

Several websites (TransUnion, Equifax, Credit Karma, Credit Sesame etc.) offer different credit scores to consumers but are not used by lenders. Innovis, ChexSystems and PRBC are other companies that produce credit scores used by some lenders.

Note: Whew scores and more scores, Here's really all you need to know. You have a VantageScore from each of the bureaus. They use the exact same formula because they all joined forces to create the formula. You would have the exact same VantageScore from each bureau if you had the same information in each bureau. Although it's highly unlikely you have the same information in all the bureaus. The VantageScore is used by only 10% of lenders.

You also a FICO score from each bureau. Used by 90% of credit lenders. This score would also be exactly the same for each bureau if you had the same information in each bureau. This again is highly unlikely.

You also have Industry Specific FICO Scores from each of the bureaus. Credit Cards, Auto Industry, Installment Loan, Personal Finance and finally Mortgage.

YOUR ALLIES THE FTC

Note: You have some pretty big Axis bullies in the playground with a lot of money (The Credit Bureaus). You also have one REALLY BIG friend that nobody wants to mess with. He's called the FEDERAL GOVERNMENT. They are the guys that if you owe money to them. Well they can seize everything you own. They are the guys that can bomb other countries. They are the guys who can send the FBI.

Have you ever noticed Post Offices don't get robbed very often. As soon as you walk into a Post Office you are on Federal land. If you rob a Post Office it's a Federal crime and some mandatory 20 years. Nobody wants a problem with the Federal Government and that includes the Credit Bureaus.

In reality it's the only thing they are scared of and rightly so. The Federal government branch that is in charge of the Credit Bureaus is called the Federal Trade Commission or FTC. The FTC created what is called the "Fair Credit Reporting Act" to keep the Bureaus in check. They are also in control of the Data Furnishers and users of credit reports (employers etc.)

My Experience: Finance Degree, 6 years loans officer at a national bank, 4 1/2 years credit bureau manager for one of the big three credit bureau's   John Harris

The "Fair Credit Reporting Act"

The Fair Credit Reporting Act, 15 U.S.C. § 1681 ("FCRA") is U.S. Federal Government legislation enacted to promote the accuracy, fairness, and privacy of consumer information contained in the files of consumer reporting agencies.

It was intended to protect consumers from the willful and/or negligent inclusion of inaccurate information in their credit reports. To that end, the FCRA regulates the collection, dissemination, and use of consumer information, including consumer credit information.

Together with the Fair Debt Collection Practices Act ("FDCPA"), the FCRA forms the foundation of consumer rights law in the United States.
It was originally passed in 1970, and is enforced by the US Federal Trade Commission, the Consumer Financial Protection Bureau and private litigants.

The Fair Credit Reporting Act, as originally enacted, was title VI of Pub.L. 91–508, 84 Stat. 1114, enacted October 26, 1970, entitled An Act to amend the Federal Deposit Insurance Act to require insured banks to maintain certain records, to require that certain transactions in United States currency be reported to the Department of the Treasury, and for other purposes.

It was written as an amendment to add a title VI to the Consumer Credit Protection Act, Pub.L. 90–321, 82 Stat. 146, enacted June 29, 1968.

Consumer Reports

Commonly referred to as credit reports, a consumer report "contains information about your credit - and some bill repayment history - and the status of your credit accounts.

This information includes how often you make your payments on time, how much credit you have, how much credit you have available, how much credit you are using, and whether a debt or bill collector is collecting on money you owe. Credit reports also can contain rental repayment information if you are a property renter.

It also can contain public records such as liens, judgments, and bankruptcies that provide insight into your financial status and obligations.

The FCRA Regulates

The FCRA regulates:

Consumer reporting agencies; Users of consumer reports; and, Furnishers of consumer information. If a consumer's rights under the FCRA are violated, they can recover: Actual or statutory damages; Attorney's fees; Court costs; and, Punitive damages if the violation was willful. "The threat of punitive damages under 1681n of the FCRA is the primary factor deterring erroneous reporting by the reporting industry."

The statute of limitations requires consumers to file suit prior to the earlier of: two years after the violation is discovered; or, five years after the violation occurred.

Consumer attorneys often take these cases on a contingency fee basis because the statute allows a consumer to recover attorney's fees from the offending party.

Users of Consumer Reports

Users of the information for credit, insurance, or employment purposes (including background checks) have the following responsibilities under the FCRA:

Users can only obtain consumer reports for permissible purposes under the FCRA; Users must notify the consumer when an adverse action is taken on the basis of such reports; and, Users must identify the company that provided the report, so that the accuracy and completeness of the report may be verified or contested by the consumer.

Employment Background checks

My Experience: Finance Degree, 6 years loans officer at a national bank, 4 1/2 years credit bureau manager for one of the big three credit bureau's   John Harris

Employers using consumer reports to screen job applicants or employees must follow specific procedures, including: Get your written permission; Tell you how they want to use your credit report; Not misuse your information; Give you a copy of your credit report if the employer decides not to hire or fires you; and, Give you an opportunity to dispute the information contained within your credit report before making a final adverse decision.

Furnishers of Information

A creditor, as defined by the FCRA, is a company that furnishes information to consumer reporting agencies. Typically, these are creditors, with which a consumer has some sort of credit agreement (such as credit card companies, auto finance companies and mortgage banking institutions).

Other examples of information furnishers are collection agencies (third-party collectors), state or municipal courts reporting a judgment of some kind, past and present employers and bonders. Lenders have an important role to play in ensuring credit reports are accurate. Under the FCRA, creditors who furnish information about consumers to consumer reporting agencies must:

Provide complete and accurate information to the credit reporting agencies;

Investigate consumer disputes received from credit reporting agencies;

Correct, delete, or verify information within 30 days of receipt of a dispute; and, Inform consumers about negative information which is in the process of or has already been placed on a consumer's credit report within one month.

(This notice doesn't have to be sent as a separate notice, but may be placed on a consumer's monthly statement. If sent as part as the monthly statement, it needs to be conspicuous, but need not be in bold type. Required wording (developed by the US Federal Treasury Department):

Notice before negative information is reported: We may report information about your account to credit bureaus. Late payments, missed payments, or other defaults on your account may be reflected in your credit report.

Notice after negative information is reported: We have told a credit bureau about a late payment, missed payment or other default on your account. This information may be reflected in your credit report.

Consumer Reporting Agencies

Consumer reporting agencies (CRAs) are entities that collect and disseminate information about consumers to be used for credit evaluation and certain other purposes, including employment. Credit bureaus, a type of consumer reporting agency, hold a consumer's credit report in their databases. CRAs have a number of responsibilities under FCRA, including the following:

CRAs must maintain reasonable procedures to ensure the maximum possible accuracy of the information contained within a consumer's report; Provide a consumer with information about him or her in the agency's files and take steps to verify the accuracy of information disputed by a consumer;

If negative information is removed as a result of a consumer's dispute, it may not be reinserted without notifying the consumer in writing within five days; and, Remove negative information seven years after the date of first delinquency (except for bankruptcies (10 years) and tax liens (seven years from the time they are paid).

Nationwide Specialty Consumer Reporting Agencies

In addition to the three big CRAs, the FCRA also classifies dozens of other information technology companies as "nationwide specialty consumer reporting agencies" that produce individual consumer reports used to make credit determinations. Under Section 603 of the Fair Credit Reporting Act, the term "nationwide specialty consumer reporting agency" means a consumer reporting agency that compiles and maintains files on consumers on a nationwide basis relating to:

Medical records or payments;
Residential or tenant history;

My Experience: Finance Degree, 6 years loans officer at a national bank, 4 1/2 years credit bureau manager for one of the big three credit bureau's John Harris

Check writing history;
Criminal background; and,
Other public record information.

Because these nationwide specialty consumer reporting agencies sell consumer credit report files, they are required to provide annual disclosures of their report files to any consumer who requests disclosure. A partial list of companies classified as nationwide specialty consumer reporting agencies under FCRA includes: Telecheck, ChoicePoint, Acxiom, Integrated Screening Partners, Innovis, the Insurance Services Office, Tenant Data Services, LexisNexis, Retail Equation, Central Credit, Teletrack, the MIB Group, United Health Group (Ingenix Division), and Milliman.

Note: Whew, ok so the "Fair Credit Reporting Act" protects the consumer (you) from all kinds of crazy things these guys try and do. This "Fair Credit Reporting Act" combined with your other Allies are going to get you great credit. For now just know that you have a friend in the Federal Government.

YOUR OTHER ALLIES THE BK BOMB

Note: I know you are thinking is claiming bankruptcy really one of your ALLIES? Well this is the big Federal Government guy helping out again. If creditors had their way you would be in debt your whole life with no way out. Bankruptcy is a great way out of certain situations. Seriously folks Creditors and Credit Bureaus **perpetuate** this myth that if you claim Bankruptcy you are done. It's all over you might as well move to Nigeria because nobody in America wants anything to do with YOU.

Then as soon as you claim Bankruptcy they start sending you credit card offers. Hey we see you claimed Bankruptcy good financial move. Now that you don't owe anyone money and can't claim Bankruptcy again for a long time, do you need a credit card?

Should You Claim Bankruptcy

The word "bankruptcy" itself sounds so ominous. The media bombards us with nightmare tales of seemingly solid business giants going from bedrock to bankrupt. The list of the bankrupt runs the spectrum from personal to corporate bringing together the likes of President Donald Trump with Sears.

Gossip columns never get tired of dishing on the latest celebrity inches from bankruptcy. You might even fear that you're a few steps from going under. After all, we live in an economy in which credit card offers clutter our mailboxes. and living in debt is an accepted norm.

Personally I love the bankruptcy option. You wipe out your debts and your credit repairs very quickly. Here is why. Your credit is a score of your ability to repay debt. If most of your debt has been wiped out you are credit worthy. I have seen it time and time again. Someone with a low score claims bankruptcy and in two years they have no debt and great credit. If bankruptcy works for you do it. Don't worry about the stigma associated with bankruptcy. Just do it. It is a rather simple process. Shop around for an affordable attorney that will take payments.

Here is the TOP SECRET FICO Point System for Bankruptcy

Months Since Bankruptcy	0 (no bankruptcy)	75 points
Months Since Bankruptcy	0-5	10 points
Months Since Bankruptcy	6-11	15 points
Months Since Bankruptcy	12-23	25 points
Months Since Bankruptcy	24+	55 points

Note: This amazes me to this day I travel the country speaking at Universities and Corporations on Credit Repair. There will always be one attendee that will ask me how much his score is going to go up

My Experience: Finance Degree, 6 years loans officer at a national bank, 4 1/2 years credit bureau manager for one of the big three credit bureau's   John Harris

because his 9 1/2 year old Bankruptcy is about to fall off his report.

Sadly I have to tell him next to nothing or more likely nothing. Look the Credit Bureaus know a Bankruptcy is a smart legal move. Once you do it you can't file again for a long time. After filing you will start getting flooded with credit offers.

Things To Consider

Here are a few questions to help you assess your financial danger zone:

Do you only make minimum payments on your credit cards?
Are bill collectors calling you?
Does the thought of sorting out your finances make you feel scared?
Do you use credit cards to pay for necessities?
Are you considering debt consolidation?
Are you unsure how much you actually owe?
Assess Your Situation

If you answered yes to two or more of the questions above, you at least want to give your financial situation a little more thought. Simply put, bankruptcy is when you owe more than you can afford to pay.

To determine where you are financially, inventory all of your liquid assets. Don't forget to include retirement funds, stocks, bonds, real estate, vehicles, college savings accounts, and other non-bank account funds.

Add up a rough estimate for each item. Then, collect and add up your bills and credit statements. If the value of your assets is less than the amount of debt you owe, declaring bankruptcy may be one way out of a sticky financial situation.

How Do You Claim Bankruptcy

You can go bankrupt in one of two main ways. The more common route is to voluntarily file for bankruptcy. The second way is for creditors to ask the court to order a person bankrupt.

There are several ways to file bankruptcy, each with pros and cons. You may want to consult a lawyer before proceeding so you can figure out the best fit for your circumstances.

Chapter 7 Bankruptcy

There are lots of reasons people file for Chapter 7 bankruptcy. Some common reasons for filing for bankruptcy are unemployment, large medical expenses, seriously overextended credit, and marital problems. Chapter 7 is sometimes referred to as a "straight bankruptcy." A Chapter 7 bankruptcy liquidates your assets to pay off as much of your debt as possible. The cash from your assets is distributed to creditors like banks and credit card companies.

Within four months, you will receive a notice of discharge. The record of your bankruptcy will stay on your credit report for ten years. But even that doesn't have to mean doom. Lots of Chapter 7 filers have bought homes with recent bankruptcies on their record. For many people like I said before, Chapter 7 offers a quick, fresh start.

But Chapter 7 bankruptcies aren't right for everyone. Almost all assets are taken and sold to repay creditors. If a debtor owns a company, a family home, or any other personal assets which he or she wants to keep, Chapter 7 may not be the best option.

Chapter 13 Bankruptcy

For people who have property they want to keep, filing a Chapter 13 bankruptcy may be the better choice.

A Chapter 13 bankruptcy is also known as a reorganization bankruptcy.

My Experience: Finance Degree, 6 years loans officer at a national bank, 4 1/2 years credit bureau manager for one of the big three credit bureau's   John Harris

Chapter 13 enables people to pay off their debts over a period of three to five years. For individuals who have consistent, predictable annual income, Chapter 13 offers a grace period. Any debts remaining at the end of the grace period are discharged.

Once the bankruptcy is approved by the court, creditors must stop contacting the debtor. Bankrupt individuals may then continue working and paying off their debts over the coming years, and still keep their property and possessions.

It can be hard to admit you need help getting out of debt, or that you can't do it alone. But that's why our government has bankruptcy laws to protect not only the creditors, but you! If you have a nerve-racking debt-load, it may be time to face financial facts. Perhaps you've been trying to ignore the ringing phone and the pile of unpaid bills that won't go away.

However, you could be doing yourself a disservice by not filing for bankruptcy. With a good lawyer and the right information, filing bankruptcy could give you the financial footing you need to get a fresh start. In other words, throwing in the towel may just be the beginning you need.

What Can You Dismiss in a Bankruptcy

Credit cards or unsecured loans.
Car repossessions and deficiency's
Some car accidents.
Material supplier debts.
Medical bills.
Lawsuits and judgments.
Evictions and unpaid rent.
Unpaid utility bills.
Foreclosure balances

What Can't You Dismiss in Bankruptcy

Taxes if they are less than 2 years old
Student loans
Alimony and child support
Debts obtained through fraud
Debts you failed to schedule in time to allow creditors to file.
Debts for fraud while you were acting in a fiduciary capacity
Debts for willful and malicious injury
Debts for fines or penalties to governmental units
Debts for judgments in wrongful death or personal injury lawsuits

The Basic of Credit Card Debt and Bankruptcy

In an economy where housing problems dominate the headlines, high interest credit cards still remain one of the largest issues consumers face in their fight for financial health. It should come as no surprise to learn then, that credit card debt is still one of the primary reasons consumers are forced to file for bankruptcy.

When a credit card account has been delinquent for more than 180 days, banks will charge off what is owed as "bad debt" and sell the account to a debt collector who will call, harass and even sue if the past due balances are high enough. Mounting pressure from debt collectors pushes many consumers through the front door of a bankruptcy office because chapter 7 protection is widely perceived as the fastest and best way to get out from under unmanageable credit card debt. While it is true that filing for bankruptcy can help discharge credit card bills, there are some basics that every consumer needs to know before relying on bankruptcy as a debt relief measure.

Credit Card Debt is Dischargeable in Bankruptcy

That's the number one rule when it comes to unsecured debts like credit cards debts and medical bills, they are dischargeable in bankruptcy. When you file for bankruptcy, all of your unsecured debts are eliminated, meaning you do not legally owe these bills any longer. Credit card companies who choose to pursue you for old, discharged debts will do so in violation of the law and will be subject to sanctions by the bankruptcy court. Furthermore, unlike debts that are forgiven through

My Experience: Finance Degree, 6 years loans officer at a national bank, 4 1/2 years credit bureau manager for one of the big three credit bureau's   John Harris

private negotiation with a lender, there is no tax liability for debts that are discharged in bankruptcy.

Your Credit Reports Should Show ZERO Balances on Your Credit Cards After Bankruptcy.

This is an area where consumers get tripped up. After bankruptcy, The credit card companies are required to report discharged debt as having a ZERO balance. It is often necessary to check your credit report and confirm its accuracy after your case closes.

Fraud Will Prevent Credit Card Debt From Being Discharged

While the general rule is that credit card debt is easily eliminated by filing for bankruptcy, fraudulent activity can jeopardize your entire bankruptcy discharge. Using credit cards for luxury purchases prior to bankruptcy creates a presumption of fraud which can be difficult to overcome. Don't use credit cards after meeting with a bankruptcy attorney unless you've decided not to file. The bottom line is any use of credit cards with the intention of not paying the debt back is fraudulent. The bankruptcy code protects debtors who behave in good faith and punish debtors who to try to game the system.

Can You Keep a Credit Card Out of Your Bankruptcy

All debts including credit card debts, must be disclosed in your bankruptcy petition. This means that you cannot keep any credit card that has a balance "out of your bankruptcy", it must be disclosed and will be discharged along with the rest of your unsecured debts. Credit cards with zero balances do not create a debt obligation and are therefore not required to be disclosed in a bankruptcy filing.

Will You Be Able to Get a Credit Card After Bankruptcy

Believe it or not yes. Creditor companies often send debtors offers for credit cards after they filed for bankruptcy knowing that it will be 8 years before they can file for bankruptcy again. Additionally, bankruptcy will illuminate all of your unsecured debt making your debt to income ratio more attractive to lenders who see that you now have the ability to take on new debt.

How Will Bankruptcy Effect Your Credit

The main issue that discourages most people from filing bankruptcy is the detrimental effect is has on their credit. It's true that a bankruptcy can stay on your credit report for up to ten years and it seriously hurts your credit score. However, not filing for bankruptcy and allowing your debts to go to collections will also severely negatively impact your credit.

Note: One 90 day late payment will have the exact same effect on your credit score as a Bankruptcy. Also realize that when you claim Bankruptcy your debts will be wiped clean which will increase your credit score.

Again here is the TOP SECRET FICO Point System for Bankruptcy

Months Since Bankruptcy	0 (no bankruptcy)	75 points
Months Since Bankruptcy	0-5	10 points
Months Since Bankruptcy	6-11	15 points
Months Since Bankruptcy	12-23	25 points
Months Since Bankruptcy	24+	55 points

The primary remedy for this is time, though there are additional measures you can take to positively enhance your credit report and score. Ultimately, if you manage your new debts well, your score will increase rapidly, and in time you will be able to run your financial life successfully, even if the bankruptcy has not yet dropped off your report.

How Long Will Bankruptcy Effect Your Credit

The bankruptcy itself and the debts associated with the bankruptcy will be displayed differently on your credit report. A completed Chapter 13 bankruptcy will stay on your report for up to seven years, and discharged debts will also stay on the report up to seven years after they are

My Experience: Finance Degree, 6 years loans officer at a national bank, 4 1/2 years credit bureau manager for one of the big three credit bureau's   John Harris

discharged. Since many debts will remain active in a Chapter 13 bankruptcy until the end of a three to five year payment plan, the debts that were discharged could actually remain on the report longer than the bankruptcy itself.

A completed Chapter 7 bankruptcy will stay on your credit report for up to ten years. Moreover, because all debts associated with a Chapter 7 bankruptcy are discharged within a few months of filing, they should drop off the report a few years before the bankruptcy itself. In general, discharged debt drops off a credit report after 7 years.

Basically, as the items on your report associated with the bankruptcy get older, they will have less and less of an effect on your credit score. This, by the way, may speak to the timeliness of filing for bankruptcy as opposed to letting collections accounts linger and then filing later.

Not Your Ally

Debt Consolidation

Note: Ok after talking about Bankruptcy we really need to talk about debt consolidation. You have all seen the nice commercials where the nice family has a new lower payment on their consolidated debt. Many of these companies have really nice names and pretend to be nonprofit. Is this the Gennie in the lamp? Just consolidate and everything will be fine.

Oh the horror stories I have heard after being in the finance business for many years. All consolidation stories have a terrible ending. Most have a terrible beginning, middle and ending.

Remember our friends at the Federal Trade Commission FTC. Here's what they say about debt consolidation:

If you feel smothered by your monthly bills, a call from someone who says they can reduce or eliminate your debts might sound like the answer to your problems. But in many cases, unscrupulous people are behind these calls. They don't have any intention of helping you, but are very interested in taking your money.

How can you tell if you're dealing with a debt relief scammer? Because they ask you to pay them before they do anything for you.

That's what the FTC and the Florida Attorney General said happened in a massive debt relief scam they were able to stop last month. The defendants told people they would pay, settle, or get rid of their debts. But they didn't. Instead, they just took people's money.

Over time, people found out that their debts were not paid, their accounts were in default, and their credit scores were severely damaged. Some people even got sued by their creditors, or were forced into bankruptcy.

Unfortunately, scammers try to take advantage of those dealing with debt but there's legitimate help out there. You can talk to your creditors directly to negotiate a modified payment plan. You also can look for credit counseling. To find reputable help, start with a credit union, local college, military base, or the U.S. Cooperative Extension Service.

Red Flags that Indicate a Debt Consolidation Scam

Before you begin comparing debt consolidation loans, make sure you understand that debt consolidation means that a company or a lender will buy all of your debt (the balance owed on your credit cards or other loans) and you will repay that company with one monthly payment, hopefully at a lower interest rate. Some indicators that the company offering to consolidate your debt is not legitimate include:

- You're told that your loan approval is "guaranteed" or "highly likely"
- You're asked for an upfront payment before the loan is approved
- You're told that this will be a "quick fix" when it will take time to repay your debt
- You're asked to provide access to your bank account so the company can make automatic withdrawals
- The contract says you can only sue the company in certain states and not the state where you live

My Experience: Finance Degree, 6 years loans officer at a national bank, 4 1/2 years credit bureau manager for one of the big three credit bureau's   John Harris

- The company only has a P.O. Box and not an office address
- The company tries to convince you to take a debt settlement rather than pay off the debt, which will hurt your credit
- Aggressively ask you to sign papers before you have had a chance to review them

Choose a Legitimate Debt Consolidation Loan Program

Before you choose a debt consolidation company, it's essential that you take the time to do your homework to avoid a scam and to get the best possible outcome for your financial health.

Check out the company's reputation with several places, including the Better Business Bureau (BBB), the state attorney general's office and your local consumer protection agency, and see if the company is registered with the National Foundation of Credit Counseling.

Do an Internet search with the company's name and the word "complaints" to see if there are customer complaints or lawsuits against them. Find out if the company is licensed to provide services in your state.

Next, research the services provided by several companies and how much they charge.

Once you have a sense of which companies offer legitimate debt consolidation services, compare specific offers from more than one company.

You'll need to do some math to decide which debt consolidation loan is best for your needs.

Note: If you want my opinion I strongly advise against debt consolidation.

Getting Your Reports and Scores

Note: Ok in order to repair and increase your credit report and score you are going to need to know what is on your report. We are also going to need to monitor your credit for improvements. You also have Allies and Axis here as well. First I need to tell you about one big joke.

The Annualcreditreport JOKE

Here is the AD they run on Google:

.www.annualcreditreport.com

Don't be fooled by look-alikes. Lots of sites promise credit reports for free. Annualcreditreport is the only official site explicitly directed by Federal law to provide them.

Here Again Let's See What The FTC Says About This Site

The Fair Credit Reporting Act (FCRA) requires each of the nationwide credit reporting companies — Equifax, Experian, and TransUnion — to provide you with a free copy of your credit report, at your request, once every 12 months. The FCRA promotes the accuracy and privacy of information in the files of the nation's credit reporting companies. The Federal Trade Commission (FTC), the nation's consumer protection agency, enforces the FCRA with respect to credit reporting companies.

A credit report includes information on where you live, how you pay your bills, and whether you've been sued or have filed for bankruptcy. Nationwide credit reporting companies sell the information in your report to creditors, insurers, employers, and other businesses that use it to

My Experience: Finance Degree, 6 years loans officer at a national bank, 4 1/2 years credit bureau manager for one of the big three credit bureau's   John Harris

evaluate your applications for credit, insurance, employment, or renting a home.

Here are the details about your rights under the FCRA, which established the free annual credit report program.

The three nationwide credit reporting companies have set up a central website, a toll-free telephone number, and a mailing address through which you can order your free annual report.

To order, visit www.annualcreditreport.com

A Warning About "Imposter" Websites
Only one website is authorized to fill orders for the free annual credit report you are entitled to under law — Annualcreditreport. Other websites that claim to offer "free credit reports," "free credit scores," or "free credit monitoring" are not part of the legally mandated free annual credit report program. In some cases, the "free" product comes with strings attached. For example, some sites sign you up for a supposedly "free" service that converts to one you have to pay for after a trial period. If you don't cancel during the trial period, you may be unwittingly agreeing to let the company start charging fees to your credit card.

Some "imposter" sites use terms like "free report" in their names; others have URLs that purposely misspell www.annualcreditreport.com
in the hope that you will mistype the name of the official site. Some of these "imposter" sites direct you to other sites that try to sell you something or collect your personal information.

Annualcreditreport and the nationwide credit reporting companies will not send you an email asking for your personal information. If you get an email, see a pop-up ad, or get a phone call from someone claiming to be from Annualcreditreport or any of the three nationwide credit reporting companies, do not reply or click on any link in the message. It's probably a scam.

Note: Ok it sounds great right? Well I worked at a Credit Bureau when the requirement to setup a website and provide a yearly free credit report was implemented. Let me tell you many a laugh was shared around the water cooler. First you get no score just a report (although of course you can purchase that along with many other services). So this forced good deed of a free report is just a great way to get you buying something. Hold on though the rabbit hole goes much deeper.

The credit bureaus were required to give free access to these reports as part reforms to the fair credit reporting act (FACTA was the specific amendment).

Whilst the credit bureaus were forced to give free access to individuals credit reports once per year, they did win one important concession. Normally when you dispute incorrect information on a credit report, the offending bureau has a period of 30 days to respond.

If the incorrect information was found on a credit report obtained through Annualcreditreport they have a period of 45 days to respond. This is terrible when it comes to disputing items on your report.

PS: With the increase to 45 days to respond you should just avoid this site altogether.

Credit Monitoring

Credit monitoring is a service that acts like a watchdog over your credit file and notifies you of any major changes to it so you are quickly alerted to any fraud on your accounts. Because the activities of fraudsters opening accounts in your name will show up first on your credit report within 30 days, especially when they fail to make payments on fraudulent accounts in your name, credit monitoring is helpful in detecting fraud on your accounts. The problem with credit monitoring is that it only catches the thievery once your accounts have already been hacked or used fraudulently and so it cannot protect your accounts from fraud or hacking.

Keeping tabs on your credit accounts will also show you your progress

My Experience: Finance Degree, 6 years loans officer at a national bank, 4 1/2 years credit bureau manager for one of the big three credit bureau's   John Harris

when trying to repair or build your credit, so credit monitoring is very helpful in knowing where your credit stands. We need to use companies that update your report. So when you get deletions you know what is going on.

More Allies CreditKarma.com

Credit Karma is an American multinational personal finance company, founded on August 16, 2006, by Kenneth Lin, Ryan Graciano and Nichole Mustard. It is best known as a free credit and financial management platform, but its features also include free tax preparation, monitoring of unclaimed property databases and a tool to identify and dispute credit report errors.

All of Credit Karma's services are free to consumers. Revenue from targeted advertisements for financial products offsets the costs of its free products and services. Credit Karma earns revenue from lenders, who pay the company when Credit Karma successfully recommends customers to the lenders.

Why Use CreditKarma.com?

Simple, Credit Karma is always 100% free and they update your report. They also have some interesting features we will talk about later.

What's the Catch?

You may be wondering, "If Credit Karma is really free, how do they make money? Do they sell my information?" No. Rest assured, they don't make money by selling your information. It's against their privacy policy

Are you going to be bombarded with ads?" Simply put, they do generate revenue through advertising partners, but it may not be the kind of advertising you imagine. Rather, their goal is to provide personalized offers that might be helpful to you based on your current credit situation.

Credit Karma recommendations are based on powerful algorithms that find products based on your credit profile. These offers may include refinancing options if you look like you might be overpaying for a loan, or credit cards that could help you optimize your savings and earnings (just to name a few). You are never under any obligation to take their offers.

More Catches

Credit Karma uses the calculation using the Vantage Score 3.0 model, like we talked about earlier these scores range from 300 to 850 like the FICO.

However these are not FICO scores. They can vary widely from the FICO. Also Credit Karma only provides scores for TransUnion and Equifax.

Note: Now this doesn't mean I don't want you to setup a Credit Karma account I do but just realize these are not actual FICO scores and many of my clients have found that out the hard way. Setup an account now.

Getting Your Experian Credit Report FreeCreditReport.com

Freecreditreport.com is part of a family of online consumer credit reporting sites belonging to ConsumerInfo.com, an Experian company. Consumer Info was founded in 1995 to give consumers quick, easy, and inexpensive access to their credit histories. It is now the leading provider of online consumer credit reports, credit scores, credit monitoring, and other credit-related information. Consumer Info provides credit monitoring to its more than 3.1 million members and has delivered more than 20 million credit reports on the web.

Note: You will be able to get your Experian report and Fico score

My Experience: Finance Degree, 6 years loans officer at a national bank, 4 1/2 years credit bureau manager for one of the big three credit bureau's   John Harris

here but with the free version it will only update monthly. Still it is a great resource to see what Experian has on your report. So create an account now.

https://www.creditsesame.com/

Credit Sesame provides you with free credit monitoring. And it's not a limited-time free offer that requires you to put a credit card on file, either!

Like the other two services listed here, Credit Sesame will only pull your information from a single credit bureau. In this case, the score is based on your TransUnion credit file, and it's based on the VantageScore 3.0.

Note: This site only does your TransUnion VantageScore and only updates monthly. Not really worth setting up if you have a CreditKarma account.

www.equifax.com/personal/

Equifax 3-Bureau credit scores are each based on the Equifax Credit Score model. Third parties use many different types of credit scores and will not use the Equifax 3-Bureau credit scores to assess your creditworthiness.

Note: This site charges $20.00 a month and has some features I like including the score estimator which is much better than most.

MyFico.com

Instantly access up to 28 of the most widely used FICO Score Versions

Note: Obviously these are your actual FICO scores but only updates monthly and is expensive ($40.00) a month. You should use this site when you are about to meet a lender. Use the free ones until then while you fix your credit.

PrivacyGuard.com

www.privacyguard.com -- Select the
"CREDIT PROTECTION" $19.99 Plan (You will NOT be billed that fee just the $1 for setting up the account -- Has a 14 day FREE TRIAL

Your CreditXpert Scores are provided by CreditXpert Inc. Although these scores are not used by lenders to evaluate your credit, they are intended to reflect common credit scoring practices and are designed to help you understand your credit. Your scores are based on information from the files at the three major credit reporting agencies.

Note: This is a great site because you will get a tri-merge credit report and scores from all bureaus. Cancel in a few days.

CreditCheckTotal.com

When you order your $1 3-Bureau Credit Report & FICO Scores, you will begin your 7-day trial membership in CreditCheck Total. If you don't cancel your membership within the 7-day trial period, you will be billed $29.95 for each month that you continue your membership. You may cancel your trial membership anytime within the trial period without charge.

My Experience: Finance Degree, 6 years loans officer at a national bank, 4 1/2 years credit bureau manager for one of the big three credit bureau's   John Harris

Note: This is a great site because you will get a tri-merge credit report and actual FICO scores from all bureaus. Cancel in a few days.

Free Fico/Vantage Scores

Many Credit Card Issuers Offer Free Credit Scores

ISSUER: American Express
FREE CREDIT SCORE TYPE: FICO Score 8
CREDITBUREAU: Experian
WHO CAN GET IT: Card Holders
WEBSITE:
https://www.americanexpress.com/us/credit-cards/features-benefits/free-credit-score/index.html

PS: If the link doesn't work do a Google search for American Express Free Credit Report

ISSUER: American Express
FREE CREDIT SCORE TYPE: VantageScore 3.0
CREDITBUREAU: TransUnion
WHO CAN GET IT: Anyone
WEBSITE:
https://www.americanexpress.com/us/credit-cards/features-

REMEMBER KEEP SAYING "I AM THE PERSON WITH GREAT CREDIT"

benefits/free-credit-score/index.html

PS: If the link doesn't work do a Google search for American Express Free Credit Report

ISSUER: Bank of America
FREE CREDIT SCORE TYPE: FICO Score 8
CREDITBUREAU: TransUnion
WHO CAN GET IT: Consumer Card Holders
WEBSITE:
https://www.bankofamerica.com/

PS: If the link doesn't work do a Google search for Bank of America Free Credit Report

ISSUER: Barclaycard
FREE CREDIT SCORE TYPE: FICO Score 8
CREDITBUREAU: Experian
WHO CAN GET IT: Consumer Card Holders
WEBSITE:
https://www.barclaycard.co.uk/personal/customer/experian-credit-score

PS: If the link doesn't work do a Google search for Barclaycard Free Credit Report

ISSUER: Capital One
FREE CREDIT SCORE TYPE: VantageScore 3.0
CREDITBUREAU: TransUnion
WHO CAN GET IT: Anyone
WEBSITE:
https://creditwise.capitalone.com/home

PS: If the link doesn't work do a Google search for Capital One Free Credit Report

ISSUER: Chase
FREE CREDIT SCORE TYPE: FICO Score 8
CREDITBUREAU: TransUnion

My Experience: Finance Degree, 6 years loans officer at a national bank, 4 1/2 years credit bureau manager for one of the big three credit bureau's   John Harris

WHO CAN GET IT: Card Holder
WEBSITE:
https://www.chase.creditviewdashboard.com/CreditView/login.page?enterprise=ChaseBankNA

PS: If the link doesn't work do a Google search for Chase Free Credit Report

ISSUER: Chase
FREE CREDIT SCORE TYPE: VantageScore 3.0
CREDITBUREAU: TransUnion
WHO CAN GET IT: Anyone
WEBSITE:
https://www.chase.creditviewdashboard.com/CreditView/login.page?enterprise=ChaseBankNA

PS: If the link doesn't work do a Google search for Chase Free Credit Report

ISSUER: CITI
FREE CREDIT SCORE TYPE: FICO Bankcard Score 8
CREDITBUREAU: Equifax
WHO CAN GET IT: Consumer cardholders (select cards)

WEBSITE:
https://www.cardbenefits.citi.com/Products/FICO-Score

PS: If the link doesn't work do a Google search for Citi Free Credit Report

REMEMBER KEEP SAYING "I AM THE PERSON WITH GREAT CREDIT"

ISSUER: Discover
FREE CREDIT SCORE TYPE: FICO Score 8
CREDITBUREAU: TransUnion
WHO CAN GET IT: For Cardholders; Experian Otherwise Anyone

PS: Do a Google search for "Discover Card Score Card"

ISSUER: Wells Fargo
FREE CREDIT SCORE TYPE: FICO 9
CREDITBUREAU: Experian
WHO CAN GET IT: Account Holders
WEBSITE:
https://www.wellsfargo.com/goals-credit/smarter-credit/credit-101/fico/

PS: If the link doesn't work do a Google search for Wells Fargo Free Credit Report

Credit Report and Score Must Do's

NOTE: Whew that's a lot of places to get your credit reports and scores. Here are the must do's for the low cost approach to credit repair. Sign up for CreditCheckTotal.com this will get your 3 FICO Scores and reports from all the bureaus. Make sure you cancel within 7 days. Sign up for CreditKarma so we can monitor TransUnion and Equifax VantageScore. Sign up for Freecreditreport.com so you can monitor Experian. Total cost $1

PS: Checking your own credit, whether you are checking your credit report or your credit score is considered a soft inquiry and does not hurt your credit score.

Credit Bureaus Are Always Gaming You

All three major credit bureaus have arbitration agreements in their terms of use,

My Experience: Finance Degree, 6 years loans officer at a national bank, 4 1/2 years credit bureau manager for one of the big three credit bureau's   John Harris

That means if you buy your credit report online and find an error on it, you can still dispute the error. However, if you disagree with how the credit bureau managed the dispute and want to take the bureau to court, the credit bureau can legally press the arbitration clause and force you to give up your right to argue your case before a jury.

That can make it much more difficult to prove your case and win substantial damages if you've been financially wronged.

In arbitration, your complaint will be handled by an individual arbitrator, appointed from an arbitration association chosen by the credit bureau, and it will be solely up to the arbitrator to decide your case. If you disagree with the arbitrator's decision, you are not allowed to appeal.

Forced arbitration clauses never help the consumer. They only help the business that does something wrong.

You NEED TO mail an opt-out letter to the Credit Bureau's within 30 to 60 days of receiving the report.

TransUnion's Forced Arbitration Terms of Service

HERE IS THE ONE TRANSUNION SNEAKES INTO THEIR TERMS OF USE:

AGREEMENT TO RESOLVE DISPUTES BY BINDING INDIVIDUAL ARBITRATION

THIS SECTION IS AN AGREEMENT TO ARBITRATE DISPUTES ("ARBITRATION AGREEMENT") THAT MAY ARISE AS A RESULT OF YOUR TRANSUNION INTERACTIVE MEMBERSHIPS, PRODUCTS OR SERVICES OR THE AGREEMENT. READ THIS SECTION CAREFULLY. YOU UNDERSTAND AND AGREE THAT BOTH PARTIES WOULD HAVE HAD A RIGHT TO LITIGATE DISPUTES THROUGH A COURT AND TO HAVE A JUDGE OR JURY DECIDE THEIR CASE, BUT BOTH PARTIES BY ENTERING INTO THIS AGREEMENT CHOOSE TO HAVE ANY DISPUTE RESOLVED

THROUGH BINDING INDIVIDUAL ARBITRATION. OTHER RIGHTS THAT YOU WOULD HAVE IF YOU WENT TO COURT MAY NOT BE AVAILABLE OR MAY BE MORE LIMITED IN ARBITRATION, INCLUDING YOUR RIGHT TO APPEAL.

RIGHT TO REJECT ARBITRATION

YOU HAVE THE RIGHT TO REJECT THIS ARBITRATION AGREEMENT, BUT YOU MUST EXERCISE THIS RIGHT PROMPTLY. You must notify us in writing within sixty (60) days after the date you click-on to "Accept" the Agreement. You must send your request to: TransUnion Interactive, 100 Cross Street, Suite 202, San Luis Obispo, CA 93401. This request must include your current username and a clear statement of your intent, such as "I reject the arbitration clause in the TransUnion Interactive Service Agreement."

Equifax's Forced Arbitration Terms of Service

HERE IS THE ONE EQUIFAX SNEAKES INTO THEIR TERMS OF USE:

AGREEMENT TO RESOLVE ALL DISPUTES BY BINDING INDIVIDUAL ARBITRATION. PLEASE READ THIS ENTIRE SECTION CAREFULLY BECAUSE IT AFFECTS YOUR LEGAL RIGHTS. THIS SECTION PROVIDES THAT EXCEPT AS PROVIDED BELOW, ANY AND ALL CLAIMS OR DISPUTES BETWEEN YOU AND US WILL BE RESOLVED BY BINDING ARBITRATION BEFORE A NEUTRAL ARBITRATOR THAT REPLACES THE RIGHT TO GO TO COURT AND MAY LIMIT YOUR RIGHTS TO DISCOVERY OR TO APPEAL. IT FURTHER PROVIDES THAT YOU WILL NOT BE ABLE TO BRING A CLASS ACTION OR OTHER REPRESENTATIVE ACTION IN COURT, NOR WILL YOU BE ABLE TO BRING ANY CLAIM IN ARBITRATION AS A CLASS ACTION OR OTHER REPRESENTATIVE ACTION. YOU WILL NOT BE ABLE TO BE PART OF ANY CLASS ACTION OR OTHER REPRESENTATIVE ACTION BROUGHT BY ANYONE ELSE.

Binding Arbitration. Either You or Equifax may, without the other's consent, elect mandatory, binding arbitration of any Claim (as defined

My Experience: Finance Degree, 6 years loans officer at a national bank, 4 1/2 years credit bureau manager for one of the big three credit bureau's   John Harris

below) raised by either You or Equifax against the other. As used in this arbitration provision, the term "Claim" or "Claims" means any claim, dispute, or controversy between You and Us regarding any aspect of Your relationship with Equifax, including but not limited to any Claim arising from these Terms of Use or arising from Your use of the Products or this Site or any information You receive from Us, whether based on contract, statute, common law, regulation, ordinance, tort, or any other legal or equitable theory regardless of what remedy is sought. Additionally, for purposes of this arbitration provision "Equifax" or "Us" will include Equifax's Suppliers, parents, subsidiaries, affiliates, successors, assigns, employees, agents, and any third party providing products, services, or benefits in connection with a Product provided to You. The term "Claim" shall have the broadest possible construction. If You or We elect arbitration, the arbitration will be conducted as an individual arbitration. Neither You nor We consent or agree to any arbitration on a class or representative basis, and the arbitrator shall have no authority to proceed with arbitration on a class or representative basis. No arbitration will be consolidated with any other arbitration proceeding without the consent of all parties. This arbitration provision applies to and includes any Claims made and remedies sought as part of any class action, private attorney general action, or other representative action. By consenting to submit Your Claims to arbitration, You will be forfeiting Your right to share in any class action awards, including class claims where a class has not yet been certified, even if the facts and circumstances upon which the Claims are based already occurred or existed. As an exception to the arbitration provision, You retain the right to pursue in small claims court any Claim that is within that court's jurisdiction and proceed on an individual basis.

Right to Opt-Out of this Arbitration Provision. IF YOU DO NOT WISH TO BE BOUND BY THE ARBITRATION PROVISION, YOU HAVE THE RIGHT TO EXCLUDE YOURSELF. Opting out of the arbitration provision will have no adverse effect on your relationship with Equifax or the delivery of Products to You by Equifax. In order to exclude Yourself from the arbitration provision, You must notify Equifax in writing within 30 days of the date that You first accept these Terms of Use on the Site (for Products purchased from Equifax on the Site). If You purchased Your Product other than on the Site, and thus these Terms of Use were mailed, emailed or otherwise delivered to You, then You must notify Equifax in writing within 30 days of the date that You receive the Terms of Use. You may opt-out by writing to Equifax Consumer Services LLC,

Attn.: Arbitration Opt-Out, P.O. Box 105496, Atlanta, GA 30348. Your written notification to Equifax must include Your name, address, and Equifax User ID, as well as a clear statement that You do not wish to resolve disputes with Equifax through arbitration.

Experian's Forced Arbitration Terms of Service

HERE IS THE ONE EXPERIAN SNEAKES INTO THEIR TERMS OF USE:

DISPUTE RESOLUTION BY BINDING ARBITRATION
PLEASE READ THIS CAREFULLY. IT AFFECTS YOUR RIGHTS.

SUMMARY:
MOST CUSTOMER CONCERNS CAN BE RESOLVED QUICKLY AND TO THE CUSTOMER'S SATISFACTION BY CALLING CIC'S CUSTOMER SERVICE DEPARTMENT AT 1-877-284-7942. IN THE UNLIKELY EVENT THAT CIC'S CUSTOMER SERVICE DEPARTMENT IS UNABLE TO RESOLVE A COMPLAINT YOU MAY HAVE REGARDING THE SERVICE, SERVICE WEBSITE, OR ITS CONTENT TO YOUR SATISFACTION (OR IF CIC HAS NOT BEEN ABLE TO RESOLVE A DISPUTE IT HAS WITH YOU AFTER ATTEMPTING TO DO SO INFORMALLY), WE EACH AGREE TO RESOLVE THOSE DISPUTES THROUGH BINDING ARBITRATION OR SMALL CLAIMS COURT INSTEAD OF IN COURTS OF GENERAL JURISDICTION TO THE FULLEST EXTENT PERMITTED BY LAW. ARBITRATION IS MORE INFORMAL THAN A LAWSUIT IN COURT. ARBITRATION USES A NEUTRAL ARBITRATOR INSTEAD OF A JUDGE OR JURY, ALLOWS FOR MORE LIMITED DISCOVERY THAN IN COURT, AND IS SUBJECT TO VERY LIMITED REVIEW BY COURTS. ARBITRATORS CAN AWARD THE SAME DAMAGES AND RELIEF THAT A COURT CAN AWARD. ANY ARBITRATION UNDER THIS AGREEMENT WILL TAKE PLACE ON AN INDIVIDUAL BASIS; CLASS ARBITRATIONS AND CLASS ACTIONS ARE NOT PERMITTED. CIC WILL PAY ALL COSTS OF ARBITRATION, NO MATTER WHO WINS, SO LONG AS YOUR CLAIM IS NOT FRIVOLOUS. HOWEVER, IN ARBITRATION, BOTH YOU AND CIC WILL BE ENTITLED TO RECOVER ATTORNEYS' FEES FROM THE OTHER PARTY TO THE SAME EXTENT AS YOU WOULD BE IN COURT.

Arbitration Agreement:
(a) CIC and you agree to arbitrate all disputes and claims between us arising out of this Agreement directly related to the Service, Service

My Experience: Finance Degree, 6 years loans officer at a national bank, 4 1/2 years credit bureau manager for one of the big three credit bureau's   John Harris

Website, or its content, except any disputes or claims which under governing law are not subject to arbitration. This agreement to arbitrate is intended to be broadly interpreted and to make all disputes and claims between us directly relating to the provision of the Service, your use of the Service Website, or its content subject to arbitration to the fullest extent permitted by law. However, for the avoidance of doubt, any dispute you may have with us arising out of the Fair Credit Reporting Act ("FCRA") relating to the information contained in your consumer disclosure or report, including but not limited to claims for alleged inaccuracies, shall not be governed by this agreement to arbitrate. The agreement to arbitrate otherwise includes, but is not limited to:

claims arising out of or relating to any aspect of the relationship between us arising out of the Service, Service Website, or its content, whether based in contract, tort, statute (including, without limitation, the Credit Repair Organizations Act) fraud, misrepresentation or any other legal theory; claims that arose before this or any prior Agreement (including, but not limited to, claims relating to advertising); claims that are currently the subject of purported class action litigation in which you are not a member of a certified class; and claims that may arise after the termination of this Agreement.

For purposes of this arbitration provision, references to "CIC," "you," and "us" shall include our respective parent entities, subsidiaries, affiliates, agents, employees, predecessors in interest, successors and assigns, websites of the foregoing, as well as all authorized or unauthorized users or beneficiaries of services, products or information under this or prior Agreements between us relating to the Service, Service Website, or its content. Notwithstanding the foregoing, either party may bring an individual action in small claims court. You agree that, by entering into this Agreement, you and CIC are each waiving the right to a trial by jury or to participate in a class action. This Agreement evidences a transaction in interstate commerce, and thus the Federal Arbitration Act governs the interpretation and enforcement of this arbitration provision. This arbitration provision shall survive termination of this Agreement.

(b) A party who intends to seek arbitration must first send to the other, by certified mail, a written Notice of Dispute ("Notice"). The Notice to CIC should be addressed to: General Counsel, Experian, 475 Anton Boulevard, Costa Mesa, CA 92626 ("Notice Address"). The Notice must describe the nature and basis of the claim or dispute and set forth the specific relief you seek from CIC ("Demand"). If CIC and you do not reach an agreement to resolve the claim within 30 days after the Notice is received, you or CIC may commence an arbitration proceeding. During the arbitration, the amount of any settlement offer made by CIC or you shall not be disclosed to the arbitrator until after the arbitrator determines the amount, if any, to which you or CIC is entitled.

You may obtain more information about arbitration from www.adr.org.

(c) After CIC receives notice at the Notice Address that you have commenced arbitration, it will promptly reimburse you for your payment of the filing fee. (The filing fee currently is $200 for claims under $10,000, but is subject to change by the arbitration provider. If you are unable to pay this fee, CIC will pay it directly upon receiving a written request at the Notice Address.) The arbitration will be governed by the Commercial Dispute Resolution Procedures and the Supplementary Procedures for Consumer Related Disputes (collectively, "AAA Rules") of the American Arbitration Association ("AAA"), as modified by this Agreement, and will be administered by the AAA. If the AAA is unavailable or refuses to arbitrate the parties' dispute for any reason, the arbitration shall be administered and conducted by a widely-recognized arbitration organization that is mutually agreeable to the parties, but neither party shall unreasonably withhold their consent. If the parties cannot agree to a mutually agreeable arbitration organization, one shall be appointed pursuant to Section 5 of the Federal Arbitration Act. In all events, the AAA Rules shall govern the parties' dispute. The AAA Rules are available online at www.adr.org, by calling the AAA at 1-800-778-7879, or by writing to the Notice Address.

All issues are for the arbitrator to decide, including the scope and enforceability of this arbitration provision as well as the Agreement's other terms and conditions, and the arbitrator shall have exclusive authority to resolve any such dispute relating to the scope and enforceability of this arbitration provision or any other term of this Agreement including, but not limited to any claim that all or any part of this arbitration provision or Agreement is void or voidable. The arbitrator shall be bound by the terms of this Agreement. Unless CIC and you agree otherwise, any arbitration hearings will take place in the county (or parish) of your billing address. If your claim is for $10,000 or less, we agree that you may choose whether the arbitration will be conducted solely on the basis of documents submitted to the arbitrator, through a telephonic hearing, or by an in-person hearing as established by the AAA Rules. If your claim exceeds $10,000, the right to a hearing will be determined by the AAA Rules. Except as otherwise provided for herein, CIC will pay all AAA filing, administration and arbitrator fees for any

My Experience: Finance Degree, 6 years loans officer at a national bank, 4 1/2 years credit bureau manager for one of the big three credit bureau's   John Harris

arbitration initiated in accordance with the notice requirements above. If, however, the arbitrator finds that either the substance of your claim or the relief sought in the Demand is frivolous or brought for an improper purpose (as measured by the standards set forth in Federal Rule of Civil Procedure 11(b), then the payment of all such fees will be governed by the AAA Rules. In such case, you agree to reimburse CIC for all monies previously disbursed by it that are otherwise your obligation to pay under the AAA Rules.

(d) The arbitrator may make rulings and resolve disputes as to the payment and reimbursement of fees and expenses at any time during the proceeding or in the final award, pursuant to applicable law and the AAA Rules.

(e) Discovery and/or the exchange of non-privileged information relevant to the dispute will be governed by the AAA Rules.

(f) YOU AND CIC AGREE THAT EACH MAY BRING CLAIMS AGAINST THE OTHER ONLY IN YOUR OR ITS INDIVIDUAL CAPACITY, AND NOT AS A PLAINTIFF OR CLASS MEMBER IN ANY PURPORTED CLASS OR REPRESENTATIVE PROCEEDING. Further, unless both you and CIC agree otherwise, the arbitrator may not consolidate more than one person's claims, and may not otherwise preside over any form of a representative or class proceeding. The arbitrator may award injunctive relief only in favor of the individual party seeking relief and only to the extent necessary to provide relief warranted by that party's individual claim. If this specific subparagraph (f) is found to be unenforceable, then the entirety of this arbitration provision shall be null and void.

(g) Notwithstanding any provision in this Agreement to the contrary, we agree that if CIC makes any change to this arbitration provision (other than a change to the Notice Address) during your membership in any credit monitoring or other product, you may reject any such change and require CIC to adhere to the language in this provision if a dispute between us arises regarding such membership product.

Opt-Out of Forced Arbitration

Opt-Out now so you can go to jury if you have to. This also makes your threats to sue real. If you threaten to sue but haven't sent in your Opt-Out letter you do not have that option and the bureaus know this fact.

Here's what you need to do:
Send the letter I provide to you
Enclose the Identification Form
Have it notarized
Send it registered mail
Keep copies and keep the mailing receipt

Identification Form:

 **My Experience**: Finance Degree, 6 years loans officer at a national bank, 4 1/2 years credit bureau manager for one of the big three credit bureau's   John Harris

On the bottom of this "ID DOCUMENT"

I declare under penalty of perjury (under the laws of the United States of America) that this identification provide is me
John Doe
Signature
Date

Identification Form Requirements

REMEMBER KEEP SAYING "I AM THE PERSON WITH GREAT CREDIT"

1) Driver License
2) Social Security card - If you are having difficulty locating your Social Security Card, your most recent W-2 form will be accepted **OR** 1st page of a tax return.
3) Proof of Address **ONLY** If your Driver License does not have your current mailing address on it- Any of the following is acceptable:
   a) Current utility bill
   b) Current cell phone bill
   c) Change of address card from DMV
   d) Voided check
   e) 1st page of a bank statement
   f) Current Lease Agreement
   g) Vehicle registration
   h) Vehicle insurance invoice

Contacting the Bureau Requirements

Send the letter I provide to you
Enclose the Identification Form
Have it notarized
Send it registered mail
Keep copies and keep the mailing receipt

NOTE: These requirements are required every time you contact the Credit Bureaus. Including when you dispute items. Never dispute online but we will talk about that later.

Opt-Out Letter

My Experience: Finance Degree, 6 years loans officer at a national bank, 4 1/2 years credit bureau manager for one of the big three credit bureau's   John Harris

Your Name
Address
City, State
Zip
SSN: 000-00-0000 | DOB: 1/1/1970
User ID: (This is your user Id for your TransUnion or Equifax or Experian account)

CREDIT REPORTING AGENCY
PO BOX ADDRESS
CITY, STATE
ZIP CODE

I have recently purchase a credit report from (TransUnion Equifax Experian) Please use this written letter as confirmation that I hereby Opt-Out and do not wish to resolve disputes with (TransUnion Equifax Experian) through arbitration.

Again: I reject the arbitration clause in the (TransUnion Equifax Experian) Interactive Service Agreement.

Thank you for noting my account.

{YOUR NAME HERE}
Signature:_____
Date: _____

IN WITNESS WHEREOF, the said party has signed and sealed these presents the day and year first above written. Signed, sealed and delivered in the presence of:
{PRINT YOUR NAME HERE} _____ Signature
STATE OF
COUNTY OF
I HEREBY CERTIFY that on this day before me, an officer duly qualified to take acknowledgments, personally appeared
{ YOUR NAME HERE }, who has produced _____ as identification and who executed the foregoing instrument and he/she acknowledged before me that he/she executed the same.
WITNESS my hand and official seal in the County and State aforesaid this _____ day of _____2016.

_____ Notary Public
Printed Name
My commission expires:

------------------End of Letter.
Now Get it Notarized

Now you need to get the letter(s) notarized. You will add a copy of your social security card and Driver License (or passport) for proof of your identity and go a notary of the public. DO NOT SIGN THE LETTERS UNTIL YOU GO TO THE NOTARY AND THEY TELL YOU TO SIGN IT.

Opt-Out Addresses

You may Opt-Out by writing to

Experian Consumer Services
Attn.: Arbitration Opt-Out
475 Anton Boulevard,
Costa Mesa, CA 92626

Equifax Consumer Services LLC,
Attn.: Arbitration Opt-Out,
P.O. Box 105496,
Atlanta, GA 30348

TransUnion Interactive
Attn.: Arbitration Opt-Out,
100 Cross Street, Suite 202,
San Luis Obispo, CA 93401.

Now Track Your letters

Now your letters are ready to send. You will send your letter WITH TRACKING Priority Mail. This is your proof that CRA's get your letter(s).

This is an absolute must. **File all your paperwork.**

NOTE: Ok so I hope you signed up for the credit report and score sites that I told you to use. Now let's look at what is on your report

My Experience: Finance Degree, 6 years loans officer at a national bank, 4 1/2 years credit bureau manager for one of the big three credit bureau's   John Harris

and what is not. It always surprises me that most people don't really know what is included and what is not.

What's on Your Credit Report

Although each credit reporting agency formats and reports this information differently, all credit reports contain basically the same categories of information.

Your social security number, date of birth and employment information are used to identify you. These factors are not used in credit scoring. Updates to this information come from information you supply to lenders.

Identifying Information

Your name, address, Social Security number, date of birth and employment information are used to identify you. These factors are not used in credit scoring. Updates to this information come from information you supply to lenders.

Trade Lines

These are your credit accounts. Lenders report on each account you have established with them. They report the type of account (bankcard, auto loan, mortgage, etc.), the date you opened the account, your credit limit or loan amount, the account balance and your payment history.

Credit Inquiries

When you apply for a loan, you authorize your lender to ask for a copy of your credit report. This is how inquiries appear on your credit report. The inquiries section contains a list of everyone who accessed your credit report within the last two years.

The report you see lists both "voluntary or soft" inquiries, spurred by your own requests for credit, and "involuntary or hard" inquires, such as when you apply for a loan and the bank runs your credit report.

Public Record and Collections

Credit reporting agencies also collect public record information from state and county courts, and information on overdue debt from collection agencies. Public record information includes bankruptcies, foreclosures, suits, wage attachments, liens and judgments.

What's Not on Your Credit Report

Prepaid Debit Cards, Checking Accounts and Debit Cards

None of these aforementioned items appear on your credit reports. Debit cards and checking accounts are really the same thing, as a debit card is like a plastic version of a paper check.

And, a prepaid debit card is really not much more than a reloadable gift card with fees.

None of the three items are a true extension of credit, as you're only able to spend money that is already either: A) loaded on the card, or B) deposited in an account with a bank or credit union.

There is considerable confusion over the prepaid debit card and credit reporting issue because some of the companies and individuals who are paid to endorse these cards suggest they will help your credit reports and scores, which isn't at all true.

In fact, the credit bureaus now have language in their reporting standards guide that addresses the issue of prepaid debit cards and

My Experience: Finance Degree, 6 years loans officer at a national bank, 4 1/2 years credit bureau manager for one of the big three credit bureau's   John Harris

credit reporting.

It reads, "Do not report prepaid credit cards/gift cards because the consumer has no credit obligation."

There is, however, one scenario when your checking account could bleed into your credit report: If you have overdraft protection in the form of an unused installment loan that loan can be reported to the credit bureaus.

Evidence That You Are Now Married

When you get married nobody in the credit industry knows about it.

The credit reporting agencies don't know about it, your credit scores don't know about it, and lenders don't know about it.

There is nothing on a credit report that appears or changes just because you've gotten married.

Now, if you choose to apply jointly with your new spouse or you otherwise co-mingle your existing debt obligations and liabilities, then eventually your credit reports will look similar to your spouse's credit reports because the data will be so similar.

NOTE: Want some great advice? Maintain credit independence even after you're married. There's no reason to co-mingle your debts and there's no reason to jointly apply for credit, except in the instance where you'll need two incomes to qualify for a loan.

Wealth Metrics

There's nothing on a credit reports that indicates your salary, your net worth, your debt-to-income ratio, or the amount of money in your wallet, 401K, IRA, SEP, Money Market, brokerage account, or any other savings account.

There is no way to presume someone's income by looking at his or her credit reports.

This shouldn't be a surprise because credit reports are supposed to tell a story about your creditworthiness, not your income.

NOTE: So this means that someone that makes $20,000 a year can have a better credit score than someone who makes $100,000 a year. The credit system needed to address everyone equally in order for it to be a usable system.

Income and other wealth metrics are measurements of capacity, or your ability to pay a bill. Credit reports and credit scores are supposed to tell a story about whether or not you'll choose to pay your bills.

Public Utilities

While there are exceptions to this rule most of the time your public utilities and medical bills do not appear on your credit reports month after month like a credit card or auto loan obligation.

If you do see a public utilities or medical bills on a credit report, they are likely there because they've gone into default and are being "worked" by a collection agency.

Categories On Your Credit Report

NOTE: Ok so we know all the things that appear on your credit report and the things that don't. Now let's look at the categories. Starting with Public Records. Any Public Record is always a negative item on your credit report.

My Experience: Finance Degree, 6 years loans officer at a national bank, 4 1/2 years credit bureau manager for one of the big three credit bureau's   John Harris

Categories-Public Records

In the past there were three types of public records that would appear in a credit report, all of them related to debts now there is only one that will show up.

Bankruptcy

Bankruptcy is the most obvious. It is a legal proceeding under which a person is provided relief from debts they are unable to pay. There are two primary forms of bankruptcy, called "chapters," because they are defined by chapters in the bankruptcy law.

Under Chapter 13 bankruptcy, a person repays at least a portion of their debts. Chapter 13 bankruptcy will remain in the credit report for seven years from the filing date.

Under Chapter 7 bankruptcy, a person does not repay any of the debts included in the filing. Chapter 7 bankruptcy remains on the credit report for 10 years from the filing date.

Court records are updated periodically, and the status of the bankruptcy, for instance that it has been discharged, will be updated automatically in the credit report.

Tax Lien

The second public record you used to see in a credit report is a tax lien. This results most commonly from failure to pay your taxes. Uncle Sam is serious about getting his taxes paid.

An unpaid tax lien will remain on a credit report for up to 10 years from the filing date. A paid tax lien is deleted seven years from the date it is paid.

Civil Judgements

Civil judgments are the third type of public record included in credit reports. A civil judgment is simply a debt you owe through the courts as a result of a lawsuit. If you have been sued and lost, you will likely owe a civil judgment. Once paid, the entry will be updated to show that fact.

The information is collected and updated regularly from the courts either by a representative of the credit reporting companies or provided directly by the court to the national credit reporting companies.

Great News About Public Records

NOTE: Ok now only Bankruptcy will show up on your credit report in public records here is why.

Major credit reporting policy changes have historically required an act of Congress to amend the FCRA. However, the most recent credit reporting settlement was reached between the 3 major credit bureaus and 31 states' attorneys general. Though this settlement did not originate at the federal level, it still introduces some landmark policy changes in the consumer's favor.

The multi-state settlement originally announced by the New York State attorney general, Eric Schneiderman, will apply to consumers living in all 50 states. Although the credit bureaus were not bound to make the policy changes for the states which were not involved in the settlement, it simply would not make sense from a procedural standpoint for the credit bureaus to have different sets of policies for consumers who reside in different states. This settlement became the National Consumer Assistance Plan (NCAP).

NCAP Settlement Details

The National Consumer Assistance Plan (NCAP) was birthed out of the multi-state settlement as the credit bureaus' vehicle to educate consumers and implement the changes agreed to under the settlement.

My Experience: Finance Degree, 6 years loans officer at a national bank, 4 1/2 years credit bureau manager for one of the big three credit bureau's   John Harris

In fact, the changes and new policies set forth in the settlement were so sweeping that the credit bureaus were given nearly 3 and 1/2 years before they were expected to have them fully implemented. In June of 2018 the final implementations of NCAP were completed.

According to the Consumer Data Industry Association, new and existing tax lien and civil judgment data must include a person's name, address and either a Social Security number or date of birth in order to be included in credit reports.

Upon implementing the NCAP enhanced standards for public records, the NCRAs removed all civil judgments and the majority of tax liens from their consumer credit reporting databases last July. Since then, TransUnion has decided to cease reporting tax lien data and to remove all remaining tax liens from our consumer credit reporting database in order to ensure compliance with the enhanced standards of the NCAP and to resolve pending litigation.

All tax liens will be removed from consumer credit reports the week of April 16, 2018. Experian and Equifax have also decided to cease reporting tax lien data and will take similar action in April 2018.

Bankruptcy public record data will continue to be reported. None of these have that information and all the Bureaus have stopped reporting all tax lien and civil judgements.

More Great NCAP News

NOTE: This NCAP thing just gets better and better for the consumer. Believe me you picked a great time to fix your credit. Here are the main benefits of the NCAP the Bureaus are required to do.

Establish National Credit Reporting Working Group to review and identify best practices.

Require all data furnishers to use the most current reporting format.

Eliminate the reporting of debts that did not arise from a contract or agreement by the consumer to pay, such as traffic tickets or fines.

Prohibit medical debts from being reported on credit reports until after a 180 day waiting period to allow insurance payments to be applied.

Remove from credit reports any previously reported medical collections that have been paid or are being paid by insurance.

Require debt collectors to include original creditor information with each account being reported for collection.

Require debt collectors to regularly update the status of unpaid debts and remove debts no longer being pursued for collection.

Monitor data furnishers for adherence to the announced reporting requirements and take corrective actions against data furnishers for noncompliance.

Eliminate any policies requiring that consumers obtain a credit report before filing a dispute.

Promote www.annualcreditreport.com on the nationwide credit reporting agencies' websites.

Provide special attention to consumers who are the victims of fraud, identity theft or who have credit information belonging to another consumer on their file.

Provide consumers who successfully dispute an error on their free annual credit report with the right to request an additional free report without waiting for a year.

Implement a process to share death notices received by consumers or their personal representatives across the three credit agencies.

Implement a process to share information across the three credit companies in situations where a data furnisher inaccurately reports a consumer as deceased.

Provide additional educational content about credit reports, and the dispute process.

Establish and complete a media campaign including public service announcements and paid newspaper, radio and television ads which promote consumers' rights to obtain their free annual credit report and

My Experience: Finance Degree, 6 years loans officer at a national bank, 4 1/2 years credit bureau manager for one of the big three credit bureau's   John Harris

encourage consumers to review their credit reports for accuracy and dispute any errors with the credit reporting agencies.

Provide additional information in consumers' dispute response letters about the dispute process, how their disputed accounts changed following their dispute, and what they can do if they are not satisfied with the outcome of their dispute.

Monitor data furnishers dispute responses and take corrective actions against data furnishers for noncompliance with their dispute investigation responsibilities.

NOTE: Whew, things are looking good. No more traffic ticket collections and the better dispute process. WOW.

Bankruptcy The Last Public Record Standing

NOTE: Ok, since Bankruptcy is the last possible public record.

Again here is the TOP SECRET FICO Point System for Bankruptcy

Months Since Bankruptcy	0 (no bankruptcy)	75 points
Months Since Bankruptcy	0-5	10 points
Months Since Bankruptcy	6-11	15 points
Months Since Bankruptcy	12-23	25 points
Months Since Bankruptcy	24+	55 points

Categories-Credit Inquiries

Hard and Soft Inquiries

Hard inquiries affect your credit scores while soft inquiries do NOT affect your credit scores.

Hard inquiries occur when you apply for new credit, such as a mortgage, car loan, or credit card. But other requests can trigger a hard inquiry, including those pertaining to a new insurance policy, job application, or cell phone. Each of these types of credit checks count as a single credit inquiry. One exception occurs when you are "rate shopping". That's a smart thing to do, and your FICO score considers all inquiries within a 45-day period for a mortgage, an auto loan or a student loan as a single credit inquiry. This same guideline also applies to a search for a rental property such as an apartment. These inquiries are usually recorded by the credit bureau as a type of real estate-related inquiry, so the FICO Score will treat them the same way. You can avoid lowering your FICO Score by doing your apartment hunting within a short period.

Soft inquiries, on the other hand, occur when a creditor checks your credit without your permission. This could be a lender with whom you've talked to for a pre-approval quote but haven't actually applied for a loan.

By doing a soft credit pull, they can give you an idea of your interest rate offer without actually having to do a hard inquiry that will affect your credit score.

Sometimes a soft inquiry might even be pulled by an existing creditor just checking on your current credit situation. Another example of a soft inquiry is a company that would like to send you a credit card or other loan offer.

PS: A FICO score does not take into account any involuntary inquiries made by businesses with whom you did not apply for credit, inquiries from employers, or your own requests to see your credit report.

Inquiries Are Removed After 2 Years

Inquiries can stay on your credit report for up to 2 years. Each time an inquiry is made, it is recorded by each of the three credit bureaus – Equifax, Experian, and TransUnion. And each time an inquiry is logged, it can potentially affect your credit score.

My Experience: Finance Degree, 6 years loans officer at a national bank, 4 1/2 years credit bureau manager for one of the big three credit bureau's   John Harris

How Do Inquiries Affect Your Credit Score

Inquiries may or may not affect your FICO score. A FICO score takes into account only voluntary inquiries that result from your application for credit. The information about inquiries that can be factored into your FICO score includes:

- Number of recently opened accounts, and proportion of accounts that are recently opened, by type of account.

- Number of recent credit inquiries.

- Time since recent account opening(s), by type of account.

- Time since credit inquiry(s).

For many people, one additional credit inquiry (voluntary and initiated by an application for credit) may not affect their FICO score at all. For others, one additional credit inquiry would take less than 5 points off their FICO score.

Inquiries can have a greater impact, however, if you have few accounts or a short credit history. Large numbers of inquiries also mean greater risk: people with six inquiries or more on their credit reports are eight times more likely to declare bankruptcy than people with no inquiries on their reports.

Top Secret Fico Point System For Hard Inquiries

PS: Remember people with six inquiries or more on their credit reports are eight times more likely to declare bankruptcy than people with no inquiries on their reports.

TOP SECRET FICO Point System for Inquiries

Number of Inquiries in Last 6 Months	0	70 points
Number of Inquiries in Last 6 Months	1	60 points
Number of Inquiries in Last 6 Months	2	45 points
Number of Inquiries in Last 6 Months	3	25 points
Number of Inquiries in Last 6 Months	4+	20 points

Categories-Collection Accounts

Note: Ugh, Collection Accounts these are the worse.

When an account becomes seriously past due, the creditor may decide to turn the account over to an internal collection department or to sell the debt to a collection agency. Once an account is sold to a collection agency, the collection account can then be reported as a separate account on your credit report.

Note: So your original bad credit card debt is showing up 120 days late and now a new bad collection account is showing up. So you have 2 bad marks for 1 debt.

Collection accounts have a significant negative impact on your credit scores.

Collections can appear from unsecured accounts, such as credit cards and personal loans. In contrast, secured loans such as mortgages or auto loans that default would involve foreclosure and repossession, respectively. Auto loans can end up in collections also, even if they are repossessed. The amount they are sold for at auction may be less than the full amount owed, and the remaining amount can still be sent to collections.

Going Into Collections

Depending on the type of debt owed, collections can affect you in different ways. If your debt is unsecured, such as credit card debt, and you default on your payments with that debt sent to collections, the credit card company would stop trying to collect the debt from you. Instead, the collections company that your debt was sent to, would pursue the debt and try to collect money from you. If your debt was secured, such as an auto loan and you default, then the lender might repossess your car, sell

My Experience: Finance Degree, 6 years loans officer at a national bank, 4 1/2 years credit bureau manager for one of the big three credit bureau's   John Harris

it at auction, and sell the remainder of debt you owe to a collections company. Lenders can collect money from debt in the following ways:

- Contact you on their own and ask for payment using their internal collection department.

- Hire a collection agency to try and collect.

- For revolving debt, such as credit card debt, the credit card company could sell your debt to a collection agency, which would then try to get the money from you.

- For installment loan debt, such as an auto loan, the lender may repossess the car, sell it auction, and then sell the remaining debt to a collection agency.

Collections Step by Step

Step by step, here's what happens when you have an account go into collection:

1. You miss or skip a credit card payment or fail to pay another type of bill, such as your phone bill or electricity bill.

2. The creditor may give you a grace period during which to make good on the bill. Typically, it takes longer than 30 days for an account to be sold to a collection agency or placed into collection status. They'll notify you, usually more than once, that you haven't paid and ask you to pay up. If you still don't pay, they can move your account into collections.

3. At that point, the original creditor could turn the collection account over to a collection agency. Typically, this occurs within a few months of the original delinquency date, and the original account may appear on credit reports as a "charge off," which essentially means the creditor has given up trying to recover the debt.

REMEMBER KEEP SAYING "I AM THE PERSON WITH GREAT CREDIT"

4. Just because the original creditor has given up, however, doesn't mean you won't hear from a collection agency. Once they receive the account from the original creditor, the collection agency is free to pursue you for all or part of the debt, provided they adhere to federal regulations governing collections.

5. If you're contacted by a collection agency, you have the right to the detailed accounting of the debt they claim you owe. Contacting a collections agency won't impact your credit report.

Virtually any type of unpaid debt can be sent to collection, including:

- Credit cards
- Student loans
- Auto loans
- Utilities
- Services
- Government
- Medical

How Long Do Collections Stay on Your Report

Collections are a continuation of debt owed and can stay on your credit report for up to 7 years from the date the debt first became delinquent and was not brought current. However, if an account were to become late today, the payments were never brought current, it was charged off as bad debt, closed and sent to collection, then the original delinquency date would be today's date.

After seven years, that negative information will automatically drop off your credit report, even if a collection agency has assumed the debt. The clock on the debt doesn't reset if it's transferred to another creditor; your

My Experience: Finance Degree, 6 years loans officer at a national bank, 4 1/2 years credit bureau manager for one of the big three credit bureau's   John Harris

original delinquency Date remains the same for both the original account and the collection agency account.

How Collections Impact Your Credit Report

Your credit report is meant to give potential lenders information on how you've used and managed your credit responsibilities with both positive and negative information. If you pay your bills on time and keep the balances on your accounts low, your responsible credit behavior will be reflected on your credit report. However, if you've paid late or skipped payments altogether, that information will also appear on your report.

A late payment on a credit report is negative, and the more recent a late payment is, the greater impact it has. Accounts that get to the collection stage are considered seriously delinquent and will have a significant and negative impact on your credit report.

Will Paying My Collection Accounts Increase My Score

In the newest versions of the FICO and VantageScore credit scores, however, paying or settling your delinquent debts, specifically those that have been sent to collections, can result in a higher credit score. Both FICO 9 and VantageScore 3.0 exclude collection accounts from score calculations once they've been paid off.

Note: Most lenders still use FICO 8 and it doesn't care one bit that you paid off a collection account. They look at it like you shouldn't of had it in the first place. When I travel the country speaking at

Universities and Corporations on Credit Repair. It really hurts when someone tells me they paid a huge collection account and their score never moved. So don't think of paying your collection accounts as a credit repair solution.

Many mortgage lenders require you pay or settle all your collection accounts before they will finance.

Categories- Accounts

Here's the meat of your report. All of your existing lines of credit are included in this section. If you've had any credit turned over to a collection agency, that'll be included, too.

Among some basic information, each account section tells you:

The status of the account: Current/open, closed, charged-off (sent to collections)

The responsibility of the account: Joint or individual

Your account balance

Your most recent payment

Past due information, if applicable

Your credit limit

Generally, your adverse accounts and good accounts will be split:

Categories- Adverse Accounts, Potentially Negative Items

These are the accounts that hurt your credit. If you have an account in this section, you might have made late payments, the balance might be outstanding, or the account may have been sent to a collection agency.

My Experience: Finance Degree, 6 years loans officer at a national bank, 4 1/2 years credit bureau manager for one of the big three credit bureau's   John Harris

Even if you are current on your payments for a credit account, it may still be included in this section of your credit report—if you had ever missed or were late on a payment."

All three credit bureaus (Experian, TransUnion and Equifax) allow you to dispute any of the accounts in this section. If the accounts are indeed adverse, they'll be removed from your report after seven years

Terms to know

Charge-off, Payment after charge-off: If the status of your account is "charged-off," this essentially means the creditor has given up on you, charging the amount off as a loss. Usually, they've sent your debt to collections. If you made a payment after a charge-off, it won't be removed from your account.

You did pay, and that's great! But that doesn't change what already happened. At one point, your debt was charged off, and your credit report is accurate in reflecting that. It'll show the charged-off debt for seven years from the date it first went into continuous delinquency.

Revolving account: If your account type is revolving, it's likely a credit card. These are accounts that you don't have to pay in full every month. You have the option to revolve your credit and pay interest on the amount you revolve.

Installment account: Usually loans. These are accounts with fixed payments over a fixed time period.

Open account: These are less common to see on your credit report. They're accounts that require you to pay the balance in full each month. A utilities company, for example.

Fixing Your Credit

Note: Ok fixing your credit is going into 3 categories here they are:

Identifying

Adding Points

Deleting Negatives

Note: Ok let's start with Identifying.

Identifying

Ok we need to identify all negative accounts. Here is the step by step process you should use.

Step 1

Note: These images are a little blurry because they are screen shots.

My Experience: Finance Degree, 6 years loans officer at a national bank, 4 1/2 years credit bureau manager for one of the big three credit bureau's   John Harris

Setup a folder on your computer called "Credit Repair" and 3 folders one for each Credit Bureau. Remember each bureau has different information.

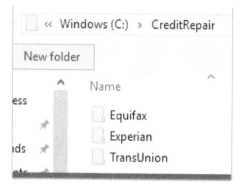

Note: Remember the 3 Credit Bureaus are all going to have different information. Here is where you have to be organized.

Step 2

Now in each folder create these folders for each Credit Bureau.

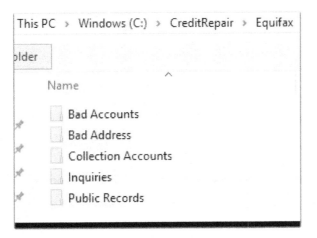

Step 3A Inquiries

Login to your CreditKarma account and take a screen shot or snipping tool of all negative items for TransUnion. Here is a sample.

Start by clicking on "TransUnion"

Now click on "Hard Inquiries"

My Experience: Finance Degree, 6 years loans officer at a national bank, 4 1/2 years credit bureau manager for one of the big three credit bureau's   John Harris

Hard inquiries

● ○ ○ **LOW IMPACT**

2

Number of times you've applied for credit

View details →

Click on "View Details"

Inquiry details

Syncb/amazon
Inquiry from Mar 10, 2017

This inquiry could stay on your report until Apr 2019.

Institution Information
Syncb/amazon
ORLANDO, FL
32896
(866) 634-8379

See an error?
Find out how to dispute a hard inquiry

REMEMBER KEEP SAYING "I AM THE PERSON WITH GREAT CREDIT"

Cap One
Inquiry from May 12, 2018

This inquiry could stay on your report until Jun 2020.

See an error?
Find out how to dispute a hard inquiry

Institution Information
Cap One
SALT LAKE CITY, UT
84130
(800) 955-7070

These both would go into your folder called "Inquiries". They should be named accordingly in this case they would be named Cap One and Syncb/amazon.

Note: All hard inquiries should be put into the folder. Regardless if you recognize them or not. When doing credit repair all negative items must be treated as disputable items. You will have to decide later if you want to dispute everything or just what you think is not yours. For now though everything negative goes into the folder.

Step 3B Public Records and Collections

Start by clicking on "TransUnion" Now click on "Derogatory Marks"

My Experience: Finance Degree, 6 years loans officer at a national bank, 4 1/2 years credit bureau manager for one of the big three credit bureau's   John Harris

Derogatory marks

●●● HIGH IMPACT

2

Collections, tax liens, bankruptcies or civil judgments on your report

View details →

Click on "View Details"

Derogatory marks

COLLECTIONS

Lvnv Funding Llc
Opened April 12, 2016

PUBLIC RECORDS

Bankruptcy
Reported on August 18, 2009

These both would go into your folders called "Public Records" and "Collections". They should be named accordingly in this case they would be named bankruptcy and Lvnv Funding.

My Experience: Finance Degree, 6 years loans officer at a national bank, 4 1/2 years credit bureau manager for one of the big three credit bureau's   John Harris

Step 3C Bad Accounts

Start by clicking on "TransUnion"

Now click on "Accounts"

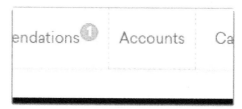

Important Note: You have to go through every OPEN and CLOSED accounts for negative accounts. This could include charge off accounts or missed payment accounts. Here are some examples.

Here is an example of an account that is current but has missed payments.

Account Details	
Account status	Closed
Type	Credit Card
Responsibility	Individual
Remarks	Charged off as bad debt
	Dispute resolved; reported by grantor

Here is an example of an account that is Charged Off as bad debt.

All these accounts should go into your folder called :Bad Accounts".

Step 3D Bad Addresses

Click on "Credit Report"

Click on "Personal Information"

"Addresses"

Screen capture any address you are not currently living at and put in folder called "Bad Addresses". When we get to the dispute process you will have to decide if you want to dispute address you actually lived.

My Experience: Finance Degree, 6 years loans officer at a national bank, 4 1/2 years credit bureau manager for one of the big three credit bureau's   John Harris

Step 4 Repeat the Process for Equifax

Step 5 Repeat the Process for Experian

This can be done here

https://www.freecreditreport.com

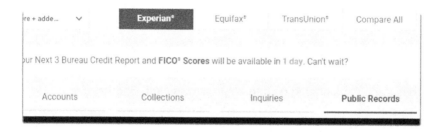

Experian has a setup very similar to CreditKarma.

Note: Wow, Ok you should have all your files full of all your derogatory credit information. Hopefully that wasn't very stressful for you. It is kind of like a blast from the past. Don't worry you are going to be the person with great credit. Now before we talk about disputing we need to talk about adding points.

Adding Points

Besides removing derogatory items (which we will talk about later) there are many ways to add points to your credit score.

Adding Points by Not Losing Points

PS: If you are trying to add points you need to know how not to lose points. So now we are going to go over how to add points and not lose points.

Don't Pay Your Bills Late From This Day Forward

Your payment history has the biggest impact on your credit score. The sole purpose of a credit score is to indicate how likely you are to repay your debt, it makes sense to look at how often you pay your bills on time. Your payment history is the most influential part of your credit score, and one missed or late payment can destroy an otherwise stellar score.

One single late payment can lower a credit score by 100 points or more. However, borrowers might be able to mitigate the damage, assuming they act fast. While missing a payment by just a few days likely won't put your scores at risk, paying bills 30 or more days late can have a serious effect on your credit.

Do whatever is necessary to avoid being late on payments. If you are forgetful, set up reminders on your phone or computer. If you spend too much, tighten your belt so you'll have the cash to make your payment.

NOTE: This is very important FICO hates late payments. Don't even try to fix your credit if you are going to continue making late payments.

My Experience: Finance Degree, 6 years loans officer at a national bank, 4 1/2 years credit bureau manager for one of the big three credit bureau's   John Harris

Don't Co-Sign on Debt

Co-signing for family or friends on their credit cards, car loans, residential leases and cellphone plans can be a quick way to ruin strong credit scores.

This can impact you negatively in two ways. First, that debt obligation can immediately show up on your credit report, and the higher debt load can impact your credit score. Second, if your friend or family member doesn't make their payments, those missed payments will show up on your credit report. If the account eventually goes to collections, that too will show up on your credit report.

NOTE: Please don't Co-Sign for anyone.

Add Rent to Your Credit Report

Note: Look if you are paying rent you should add it to your report.

Experian, Equifax and TransUnion do include rent payment information in credit reports if they receive it.

Although rent is reported as a "tradeline" on credit reports much like a mortgage or car loan would be it's not treated the same for credit scoring purposes.

The most commonly used versions of the FICO score don't use rental payment information in calculating scores, but FICO 9 and FICO XD do, as does VantageScore.

Having rental payment information in your credit report can be useful if you rent again. Landlords prefer tenants who can show a history of paying on time.

REMEMBER KEEP SAYING "I AM THE PERSON WITH GREAT CREDIT"

NOTE: Many of these companies that report your rent do so only to one bureau. This is not even worth doing.

NOTE: Also none of these companies report late or missed payments. which is great. This is because the Credit bureaus will not accept derogatory information when it comes to rental payments. The reason for this is that you might of paid the landlord directly. Here are the players in the rent reporting industry and my advice.

Rent Reporters: There is a one-time enrollment fee of $94.95, which includes up to two years of reported rental payments, then the service is $9.95 per month. It reports to TransUnion.

PS: Don't use them they only report to TransUnion.

Rental Kharma: Initial setup is $25, and the service is $6.95 per month. During enrollment, you can report payments made in the previous 24 months for a fee of $5 per month reported. It reports to TransUnion.

PS: Definitely Don't use these guys they do bad business and they only report to TransUnion.

ClearNow: This service debits your rent from your checking or savings account. There's no cost to tenants, but your landlord must be signed up. If you opt in, payments are reported to Experian.

PS: Don't use they only report to Experian.

PayYourRent: Variable fees, depending on how rent is paid; in some cases, the fees are paid by management. It reports to all three credit bureaus.

PS: Possibly use they report to all bureaus.

My Experience: Finance Degree, 6 years loans officer at a national bank, 4 1/2 years credit bureau manager for one of the big three credit bureau's   John Harris

eRentPayment: Tenants may sign up for this rental payment service only if the landlord is registered. There is a $3 per transaction fee for processing electronic rent payments; the landlord may split that cost or require that the tenant pay it. Reports to all three credit bureaus.

PS: Possibly use they report to all bureaus but landlord must be signed up to the service.

RentTrack: Fees can vary depending on whether your landlord is a client. Without landlord participation, RentTrack collects the rent for a $6.95 fee and then sends a check to your landlord. A look-back of up to 24 months is available on your current lease.

PS: These guys are the best. You can sign up even if your landlord is not signed up. They report to all the bureaus.

Rent Track

Rent payments will show up on your credit report as another account. It appears just like a charge card or mortgage, with one key difference: you don't need to take on more debt to get the credit you should already be earning.

With each payment, you receive a positive mark on your credit report – the longer you demonstrate responsibility, the better your credit.

Your rental payment information will be included as part of your standard credit report. Your positive rental payment data allows you to establish or build credit history.

Your report shows your rental property details and how much your monthly rent payment is. This updates monthly.

Your rental tradeline is used in different scoring models, such as FICO 9 score and VantageScore, and is also accepted by Fannie Mae and Freddie Mac for mortgage decisions.

Add All Your Good Standing Accounts To All Your Reports

Now check all your reports and make sure all off your reports are showing all your good accounts. Your good accounts might only be showing on one or two bureau's. You need to add these accounts to all the credit Bureaus. If you find any of these accounts here is how to add the good account.

Enclose any documentation that verifies information you're providing.

My Experience: Finance Degree, 6 years loans officer at a national bank, 4 1/2 years credit bureau manager for one of the big three credit bureau's   John Harris

Sample Add Account Letter

To Whom It May Concern

,According to the Fair Credit Reporting Act, 15 USC section 1681i, I request that you add the following credit accounts to my credit report:

Company Name
: [Name of Company]

Account Number
: [Account Number]

Account Type
: [Account Type]

Phone Number
: [Phone Number]

Date
: [Date]

I appreciate your attention to this matter, Please inform me within the statutory 30-day time period from your receipt of The purpose of this credit repair letter of your compliance with the provisions described in 15 USC 1681e,which require that all information in a consumer's credit report must reflect the maximum possible level of accuracy".

[Name]
Social Security Number: [Social Security Number]
Date of Birth: [Date of Birth]
[Current Address]:[City, State Zip]Sincerely,

[Signature]
[Date
IN WITNESS WHEREOF, the said party has signed and sealed these presents the day and year first above written. Signed, sealed and delivered in the presence of:
{PRINT YOUR NAME HERE} _____ Signature
STATE OF
COUNTY OF
I HEREBY CERTIFY that on this day before me, an officer duly qualified to take acknowledgments, personally appeared
    {   YOUR   NAME   HERE   },   who   has   produced _____ as identification and who executed the foregoing instrument and he/she acknowledged before me that he/she executed the same.
    WITNESS my hand and official seal in the County and State aforesaid this _____ day of _____2016.

_____ Notary Public
Printed Name
My commission expires:

-------------------End of Letter.
Add Your Identification Form

REMEMBER KEEP SAYING "I AM THE PERSON WITH GREAT CREDIT"

Identification Form:

On the bottom of this "ID DOCUMENT"

I declare under penalty of perjury (under the laws of the United States of America) that this identification provide is me
John Doe
Signature
Date

My Experience: Finance Degree, 6 years loans officer at a national bank, 4 1/2 years credit bureau manager for one of the big three credit bureau's   John Harris

Identification Form Requirements

1) Driver License
2) Social Security card - If you are having difficulty locating your Social Security Card, your most recent W-2 form will be accepted **OR** 1st page of a tax return.
3) Proof of Address **ONLY** If your Driver License does not have your current mailing address on it- Any of the following is acceptable:
    a) Current utility bill
    b) Current cell phone bill
    c) Change of address card from DMV
    d) Voided check
    e) 1st page of a bank statement
    f) Current Lease Agreement
    g) Vehicle registration
    h) Vehicle insurance invoice

Contacting the Bureau Requirements

Send the letter I provide to you
Enclose the Identification Form
Have it notarized
Send it registered mail
Keep copies and keep the mailing receipt

Now Track Your letters

Now your letters are ready to send. You will send your letter WITH TRACKING Certified Mail. This is your proof that CRA's get your letter(s).

This is an absolute must. File all your paperwork

Here are the addresses you need to send the letters.

Equifax
P.O. Box 740256 Atlanta, GA 30374-0256
Experian
P.O. Box 2106 Allen, TX 75013
TransUnion
P.O. Box 34012 Fullerton, CA 92634

Paying Off The Wrong Debt

Paying down your balances will improve your credit score. How much of an improvement you see depends on which debt you pay.

For example, you won't see much of an increase if you pay off an auto loan. You might see a decrease actually in your score because your loan is closed. Also credit utilization on installment loans, such as car loans, isn't weighed as heavily in credit scoring as your utilization of revolving credit.

If you would have put the money on paying down your credit card balances it would have made a huge difference.

Add 1 or Preferably 2- Low Amount Secured Loans

NOTE: This is a fantastic way to jump your score like crazy. Seriously folks. This first option (SelfLender.com) will cost you $12.00 up front and will show up as an installment loan from a bank. You choose between a few payment choices $24, $48, $100 that goes into an account. You even choose the length of loan. Once the term is up you get all the money back.

PS: Here is why this works so well. This will add installment loans from Banks to your credit profile. FICO doesn't care about the amounts of the loans, because remember FICO is setup to judge credit worthiness not income. Also FICO doesn't care if the loan is secured or unsecured. It only cares about the payments.

My Experience: Finance Degree, 6 years loans officer at a national bank, 4 1/2 years credit bureau manager for one of the big three credit bureau's   John Harris

SelfLender.com

Traditionally, consumers with bad or no credit histories were relegated to high-fee loans or credit cards that provided minimal help to their credit-building journey. Those substandard options are changing as Fintech companies leverage advances in technology to create consumer products with lower fees and greater impact on credit scores.

A Credit Builder account through SelfLender includes an installment loan for between $500 and $1,700. The money from the loan is placed in a certificate of deposit (CD) in the customer's name, and monthly loan payments are reported to three credit bureaus. Once the loan is paid off, in 12 to 24 months, the CD is closed and a check for the full amount, including interest earned, is sent to the customer. Average credit score gains from the service have ranged between 40 and 100+ points.

PS: If you don't have a lot of money choose the lowest payment option it will increase your credit score the exact same as a higher payment. Also Self Lender doesn't do a credit check (yeah you heard me right no credit check).

PSS: Make sure you make your payment because if you go 30 days late it will report negative. If you can't make the payment call SelfLender before the 30 days.

Second Secured Loan

Unfortunately SelfLender only allows you to have one loan at a time. So you should get a second one at a Credit Union. The only problem is unlike SelfLender you will need to deposit the amount of the loan in an account. Do a search for banks that offer secured loans. Take out the lowest amount possible. Many have $500 options.

Department Store Cards UGH

A retail credit card from your favorite store is enticing. If you enjoy shopping and the ability to finance your purchases, you might find yourself eager to submit the application. You don't need perfect credit to get approved for a retail credit card, which can make applying even more tempting. Some store cards will approve applicants with scores as low as 550, which is considered poor.

Typically, retail credit cards have more relaxed qualification requirements. If you are just building your credit, you might think you want to start with a retail card. Retail cards with a Visa or MasterCard affiliation are issued by a bank instead of the store's financing department. For example, Capital One issues the Saks Fifth Avenue credit card and Citibank issues the Sears card (before the bankruptcy). These stores tend to follow the issuing bank's underwriting criteria.

Credit card issuers do not specify the average score necessary to obtain a retail credit card. There is no defined range for a fair credit score, but typically a FICO score between 580 and 669 are considered fair. For a Walmart credit card, a score of 660 or higher is recommended, but those with scores as low as 550 have reported success when applying for the card. Best Buy credit cards, which are issued by Citibank, require a credit score of at least 660.

Retail credit card companies consider more than a credit score when reviewing applications. Your employment status, ability to pay, willingness to pay and credit score are all factors used to determine approval. A person with a low credit score because of lack of credit could be more likely to gain approval than an applicant who has a low score because of missed payments or an account in collection.

If a store chooses to extend you credit, your credit score and income are generally used to calculate your credit limit. Credit card companies may increase your limit after you display a dependable payment history. The economy also plays a role in your ability to qualify for a retail credit card. Creditors tend to tighten lending standard in a sluggish economy. When the economy is booming, standards are often more relaxed.

My Experience: Finance Degree, 6 years loans officer at a national bank, 4 1/2 years credit bureau manager for one of the big three credit bureau's   John Harris

A retail credit card has many disadvantages for consumers with established credit. Retail credit cards often carry higher interest rates. Simply applying for a retail credit card can hurt your score. Every application you submit appears on your credit report as an inquiry.

Retail credit cards tend to have lower limits, even an inexpensive purchase can generate a high credit-utilization ratio. Your utilization ratio is calculated by comparing the balances on your credit cards with the credit limits.

NOTE: Look I am going to be completely honest with you FICO hates department store cards. People that use these types of cards are prone to default. People that have good credit don't use these types of cards because of the high interest rates. Don't get a department store card.

The Almighty Credit Card

NOTE: Credit Cards are a major factor in your FICO Score. Did I say major I meant MAJOR FACTOR.

Having No Credit Cards

Lenders like to see a long history of responsible credit use, and if you don't have a card, you might not have much information to show. Although it seems counterintuitive, not having any credit cards will actually hurt your credit score as much as having too many. You need credit cards in order to have a high FICO it's that simple.

You might be thinking well I can't get approved for a credit card. Yes you can and we will talk about that a little later.

How Many Cards Should You Have

TOP SECRET FICO Point System for Credit Cards

Number of Bank Card Tradelines	0	15 points
Number of Bank Card Tradelines	1	25 points
Number of Bank Card Tradelines	2	50 points
Number of Bank Card Tradelines	3	60 points
Number of Bank Card Tradelines	4+	50 points

NOTE: So the ideal number of credit cards is 3. This really shouldn't be surprising because the average American has 3.2 credit cards

Getting Secured Credit Cards

NOTE: So the ideal number of credit cards is 3 but that doesn't mean you should just blindly start applying for credit cards. This will only lead to frustration. Never apply for a credit card unless you know your FICO BANKCARD 8 SCORE from all three credit bureaus. We will talk about that a little later but for now let's start at the beginning with "Secured Credit Cards".

What is a Secured Credit Card

The biggest difference between a secured and an unsecured credit card is that secured cards typically require a security deposit from the cardholder, which functions as cash collateral against you defaulting on your payments.

Secured credit cards are especially useful for consumers with poor or little to no credit history who are typically declined for unsecured credit cards. A secured card can almost guarantee approval by the lending institution because, in effect, you are the one taking on the financial risk through your security deposit.

My Experience: Finance Degree, 6 years loans officer at a national bank, 4 1/2 years credit bureau manager for one of the big three credit bureau's   John Harris

Think of a secured card as your credit line "training wheels" that allow you the benefits of owning a credit card while giving you the opportunity to build a history of responsible credit use with on-time payments. The small credit limits and security deposit requirements are there to protect you from getting yourself into the poor payment history that may have plagued you in the past.

Secured card credit limits are often set at the amount of the security deposit or some percentage of it so that you cannot charge more than your security deposit can cover. Depending on your specific secured card, adding more to your security deposit enables you to access a higher credit limit, or if your payments are on-time and consistent, the credit card company may reward you by increasing your credit line without requiring additional deposits.

Many secured cards increase the credit limit of your secured card after 6-12 months of responsible use and on-time payments.

How Does FICO View A Secure Credit Card

Just like the secured loan we talked about earlier the FICO score doesn't care that it's reported as secured. The score sees it as a credit card. Your credit limit and your utilization ratio are considered in the calculation. But the FICO score doesn't take off points because you're using secured credit cards.

The score really detests late payments and high utilization ratios, though, so use the card responsibly and keep your balances low. So in reality if you had 3 secured credit cards you would have the best possible FICO score in that calculation.

Three Things That Matter In A Secure Credit Card

1) Will you get approved. Yes you can get denied and many people do get denied every year. This sounds crazy but it's true. The reason for this is the issuing bank just doesn't think you will make payments. They just don't want to be bothered with all the hassle. Most secured cards run a credit check.

2) Do they run a credit check. There are some that don't so you won't be denied.

3) Will the secured card become a non-secured card at some point.

Secured Cards You Need

NOTE: Here is a list of secured cards how they report and if they turn into non-secure cards

Capital One Secured MasterCard Credit Card
Credit bureaus: Reports as unsecured.
Graduate to non-secured: Yes
Easy To Get: Yes

NOTE: This should be your first Secured Card.

Open Sky Secured Credit Card
Credit bureaus: Reports as unsecured.
Graduate to non-secured: No
Easy To Get: Very Easy No Credit Check

NOTE: If you have really bad credit you should get this card there is **no credit check** but will not turn into unsecured but that's ok. There is a $35 annual fee. This should be first or second card.

My Experience: Finance Degree, 6 years loans officer at a national bank, 4 1/2 years credit bureau manager for one of the big three credit bureau's   John Harris

Citi Secured Mastercard

Credit bureaus: Reports as secured.
Graduate to non-secured: No
Easy To Get: No

NOTE: Goes to unsecured after 18 months

First Progress Platinum Elite MasterCard Secured Credit Card

Credit bureaus: Reports as unsecured.
Graduate to non-secured: No
Easy To Get: Very

Primor Secured Visa Classic Card

Credit bureaus: Reports as unsecured.
Graduate to non-secured: No
Easy To Get: Very

Navy Federal Credit Union Rewards Secured Card

Credit bureaus: Reports as unsecured.

NOTE: To be eligible for this card, you have be in the military or related to someone who is.

Wells Fargo Secured Card

Credit bureaus: Reports as secured.
Graduate to non-secured: Yes
Easy To Get: Hard

BankAmericard Secured Credit Card

Credit bureaus: Reports as secured.
Graduate to non-secured: Yes
Easy To Get: Medium

U.S. Bank Secured Visa Card
Credit bureaus: Reports as secured.
Graduate to non-secured: Yes
Easy To Get: Medium

AeroMexico Visa Secured Card
Credit bureaus: Reports as secured.
Graduate to non-secured: No
Easy To Get: Easy

Merrick Bank's Secured Visa Card
Credit bureaus: Reports as secured.
Graduate to non-secured: No
Easy To Get: Easy

Non-Secured Cards Basics

NOTE: Ok, look CreditKarma and especially Credit Sesame are going to be trying to get you to apply for all kinds of cards. You don't want to apply and get the hard inquiry if you are not going to get approved.
Before applying go to creditcards.com's "CardMatch" and get preapproved. They will only do a soft inquiry.

NOTE: Never apply for a credit card unless you know your FICO BANKCARD 8 SCORE from all three credit bureaus. You can get your score at https://www.freecreditreport.com/ sign up for the monthly and then cancel. They have a section called "more FICO's" You will be able to get your BANKCARD 8 SCORE. This is the score the credit card companies will pull.

PS: Remember the magic number is 3

My Experience: Finance Degree, 6 years loans officer at a national bank, 4 1/2 years credit bureau manager for one of the big three credit bureau's   John Harris

TOP SECRET FICO Point System for Credit Cards

Number of Bank Card Tradelines	0	15 points
Number of Bank Card Tradelines	1	25 points
Number of Bank Card Tradelines	2	50 points
Number of Bank Card Tradelines	3	60 points
Number of Bank Card Tradelines	4+	50 points

Also a lender is going to consider several key factors when you apply for credit. These may include:

- **Your credit history (obviously):** While a credit score might be considered, lenders will look at all three of your credit reports to make sure you have a history of on-time payments. Depending on the card you're applying for, the issuing bank may want to see several years of on-time payments. Looking at a credit report gives the lender a more detailed picture of your financial history than a single credit score number can.

- **Your income:** This isn't on credit reports, but credit applications always ask how much you make each year. The credit card issuer wants to make sure you have steady income before extending you a line of credit. Sometimes, the bank will ask for additional documents, like tax returns, to support the annual income you write on the application. Your income can be a big factor in the credit limit you're granted by the issuer.

- **Your monthly housing cost:** Credit card applications often ask about your housing situation: whether you rent or own, and what your monthly payment is. If your monthly housing expense seems high relative to your income, that may keep a bank from approving you for new credit or factor into the terms.

Non-Secured Cards

NOTE: I would give you the links but they change all the time. Simply do a google search for the card name or go to creditcards.com. Always do the "CreditMatch" option so you only do a soft pull on your credit.

Capital One Platinum Credit Card

Credit Recommended FICO BANKCARD 8: 580-740
Annual Fee: 0

Capital One QuicksilverOne Cash Rewards Credit Card

Credit Recommended FICO BANKCARD 8: 580-740
Annual Fee: $39

Credit One Bank Platinum Visa with Cash Back Rewards

Credit Recommended FICO BANKCARD 8: 580-740
Annual Fee: $0-$99

Credit One Bank® Platinum Visa® for Rebuilding Credit

Credit Recommended FICO BANKCARD 8: 580-740
Annual Fee: 0-$99

Fingerhut Credit Account issued by WebBank

Credit Recommended FICO BANKCARD 8: 580-740
Annual Fee: 0

Milestone® Gold Mastercard®

Credit Recommended FICO BANKCARD 8: 580-740
Annual Fee: $35-$99

Credit One Bank® Unsecured Platinum Visa®

My Experience: Finance Degree, 6 years loans officer at a national bank, 4 1/2 years credit bureau manager for one of the big three credit bureau's   John Harris

Credit Recommended FICO BANKCARD 8: 580-740
Annual Fee: 0-$99

Avant Credit Card

Credit Recommended FICO BANKCARD 8: 580-740
Annual Fee: $29

Milestone® Mastercard®

Credit Recommended FICO BANKCARD 8: 580-740
Annual Fee: $35-$99

Credit One Bank® NASCAR® Visa® Credit Card

Credit Recommended FICO BANKCARD 8: 580-740
Annual Fee: 0-$99

Credit Card Holders

If You Have Credit Cards Don't Close Old Accounts

Although it's smart to limit the number of credit cards you have at any given time closing old or inactive cards can come back lower your credit score. The length of your credit history affects 15 percent of your score.

This is why it's important not to close credit card accounts that you have had for years.

Don't Consolidate Debt Onto One Card

If you owe money on several credit cards, you might be tempted to consolidate debt by transferring all the balances to one new card. But that can be a mistake. Not only can this lower the average age of your credit history, especially if you choose to close out the other cards, but it can also increase your debt-to-credit ratio.

Important Things You Need To Know About Credit Card Debt

TOP SECRET FICO Point System for Credit Cards

Average Balance on Revolving Tradelines points	No Tradelines	30
Average Balance on Revolving Tradelines points	$0	55
Average Balance on Revolving Tradelines points	$1-$99	65
Average Balance on Revolving Tradelines points	$100-$499	50
Average Balance on Revolving Tradelines points	$500-$749	40
Average Balance on Revolving Tradelines points	$750-$999	25
Average Balance on Revolving Tradelines points	$1000 or more	15

NOTE: Ok, so here's the deal with credit card balances. The lower the better but something is better than zero. This applies for each individual card that you have. FICO hates zero balances. The best FICO score you can have with credit cards is 1% on all your cards. Funny but absolutely true.

My Experience: Finance Degree, 6 years loans officer at a national bank, 4 1/2 years credit bureau manager for one of the big three credit bureau's   John Harris

Decrease your Credit Utilization

Credit use ratio accounts for 30% of your score or SO IMPORTANT. Here is how it works. Now let's look a 2 different people

John Doe and Peter Smith.

They have exactly the same items on their credit reports except. John has a credit card with a limit of $10,000. On the card he owes $7000. He has a great job making $125,000 a year and pays on time every month.

Peter has the exact same items on his credit but he has a credit card from the same company but his limit is $1000 because he is unemployed. He owes $100 on it and pays on time every month.

Who has a much better score?

Its Peter because of the Credit Utilization. He is only using 10% of his available credit. While John is using 70%.

This is so important with your FICO Score. It means so much I have to stress this point. It makes up 30% or more of your score.

Credit Utilization Components

The credit utilization category has six subcomponents

The Amount Of Debt Still Owed Lenders

The Number Of Accounts With Debt Outstanding

The Amount Of Debt Owed On Individual Accounts

The Lack Of Certain Type Of Loans (Installment loans)

The Percentage Of Credit Line Use On Revolving Accounts

The Percentage Of Debt Still Owed On Installment Loans

It's the comparison of amount of debt to the credit limit that is crucial.

That ratio goes by several names credit utilization ratio, credit-limit-to-debt ratio, balance-to-limit ratio and debt-to-available-credit ratio among them

the math is simple. It's the percentage of how much you owe compared to the amount of your credit limit. If you owe $100 on your credit card and

My Experience: Finance Degree, 6 years loans officer at a national bank, 4 1/2 years credit bureau manager for one of the big three credit bureau's   John Harris

have a $1,000 credit limit on it, your ratio is 10 percent.

Simple, right? Not always. Here's where it gets tricky:

First of all, FICO doesn't view all account types as being equal. Revolving balances (e.g., credit and retail cards) tend to carry more weight than installment debt (e.g., mortgage, auto and student loans) when amounts owed are considered.

That means that within the amounts owed category, credit cards are the most important type of account for achieving a high FICO score, but they can also do more damage than other types of credit.

Additionally, while you might consider closing an unused or unwanted credit card to be a smart financial decision, because of the way your utilization ratio is calculated, the FICO score doesn't see it that way.

As an example, imagine you have two credit cards, each with a $500 credit limit, for total available credit of $1,000.

One of the cards hasn't been used for a while and has a zero balance, while the other card has a balance of $250. That gives you a utilization ratio of 25 percent -- your $250 balance divided by your total $1,000 credit limit. You then close that unused card, eliminating the $500 credit limit associated with that account. Now, you've only got $500 in total credit available on that one card, but you still have $250 in debt.

Suddenly, your credit utilization ratio has jumped to 50 percent.

That change can drag down your FICO score despite your good intentions. People think closing your cards was always a good thing.

However, when it comes to credit scoring, Common sense doesn't always work.

It's not only your own actions that can change that utilization ratio for the worse. The bank may also take steps that have a negative impact on a cardholder's FICO score.

Some people have seen a score go down because an issuer had cut a credit line or closed their card for nonuse.

As in the example above, those changes can make it look like the borrower is closer to maxing out their line of credit, which can weigh on a borrower's FICO score.

Ace Your Credit Utilization

To improve the amounts owed portion of your FICO score, start by finding out how much credit you have available. Then, pay down balances. If you're a good customer, the banks may also grant requests to increase your revolving credit lines. An old rule of thumb used to say keep your credit utilization below 30 percent, but that's a myth. There's no magic about 30 percent. Your score won't plummet at 31 percent or soar at 29 percent. The real rule? The lower the utilization, the better but something is better than zero.

That can be especially tough for borrowers who only have one account. If you've got one credit card with a $1,000 line, it's not that hard to hit 30 percent, since you'd only need to carry a balance of $300.

But if you max out a credit card account by using up an entire line of credit, expect your FICO score to drop by 50 to 80 points.

Another danger comes from joint account holders or authorized users who put excessive charges on your shared card. If the other cardholder maxes out a shared account, your FICO score will fall.

Another recommendation is consider making payments to creditors more than once each month. Otherwise, if you put a major expense like a new appliance on a credit card, even if you plan to pay it off, your FICO score may take a hit. The reason is that credit scores are calculated as a snapshot in time, so if that happens to be right after you charged a new $1000 washing machine, your utilization ratio will look worryingly high.

Things To Do For Best Credit Utilization

My Experience: Finance Degree, 6 years loans officer at a national bank, 4 1/2 years credit bureau manager for one of the big three credit bureau's   John Harris

Pay Down Your Credit Cards

The simplest but perhaps most difficult way to lower your utilization ratio is to pay off your debt. For example, Dan has an outstanding balance of $5,000 with a $12,000 credit limit. He managed to pay off $3,000, thereby reducing his utilization ratio from 41.6 to 16.6 percent. Attacking your debt is a quick solution, but it may not be plausible for everyone.

Increase Your Credit Limit

If paying down debt isn't an option, contact your creditor and ask them to conservatively increase your credit limit. For example, if Dan increased his total credit limit to $14,000, his initial ratio would be reduced from 41.6 to 35.7 percent. By increasing your credit limit, your utilization ratio will reduce automatically.

Apply for A New Credit Card

Apply for a new credit card if you get approved you will immediately increase your ratio. Do not apply for a credit card if you have just missed some payments recently.

NOTE: Remember never apply for a credit card unless you know your FICO BANKCARD 8 SCORE from all three credit bureaus. You can get your score at https://www.freecreditreport.com/ sign up for the monthly and then cancel. They have a section called "more FICO's" You will be able to get your BANKCARD 8 SCORE. This is the score the credit card companies will pull.

Get A Home Equity Line Of Credit

A home equity line of credit (often called HELOC and pronounced Hee-lock) is a loan in which the lender agrees to lend a maximum amount within an agreed period (called a term), where the collateral is the borrower's equity in his/her house (akin to a second mortgage). The rates for these are extremely low. Your credit will sky rocket. You only pay interest on money that you use. Go to lendingtree.com and shop for the best rate.

Buying A House

Now let's say you are buying a house and have $25,000 down and have credit cards that are maxed out with a $5000 limit. You are ten times better to pay your cards down to $50.

Put down $20,050 on the house instead. Your FICO will sky rocket and you will get a much better interest rate.

Personal Loan To Pay Off Credit Cards

If you are struggling to make the payments, or if repayment is difficult due to high interest fees, taking out a personal loan with a lower interest rate and using it to pay off the credit card balance in full may be a good option. If you qualify for a loan with a low interest rate, it could mean lower payments, which can make it easier to ensure all your payments are made on time.

It may also mean you will have more money left over to put towards the loan balance in order to pay the loan off more quickly, or to use towards making sure your other bills are paid on time as well. Whatever you do get your credit card balances low.

Get Added As An Authorized User

A "piggybacker," more commonly known as an "authorized user," is a

My Experience: Finance Degree, 6 years loans officer at a national bank, 4 1/2 years credit bureau manager for one of the big three credit bureau's   John Harris

person permitted to use a credit card by a primary cardholder who maintains responsibility for all debt on the card, regardless of who makes the charges. Authorized users are typically -- though not always, as you'll see -- a spouse, partner, child, relative or friend of the primary account holder.

The term "piggybacking" refers to the way in which the entire credit history of an account is not only included in the primary cardholder's credit report and score, but also becomes part of the authorized user's report and score. this happens whether the card is actually used by the authorized user or not.

In recent years, piggybacking has become one of the more popular, and at the same time controversial, ways of building credit for someone who is either new to credit or recovering from financial setbacks. Popular, due to the ease with which an authorized user can be added to an account no credit requirements and the immediate scoring benefit that can be realized from the primary cardholder's (hopefully) positive credit history. Controversial, in that someone who has not used, not managed, or has even misused credit in the past, can reap the scoring benefit of a seasoned and well-managed card without having truly done anything to earn the additional scoring points that can accompany the account.

For example, a young person piggybacking on a parent's long-held and well maintained card can, without having any credit of her own, achieve a very good credit score based on a credit history older than she!

But, the piggybacking picture is not all win-win for authorized users.

Since the card history -- good or bad -- is included in the authorized user's credit report and credit score, it behooves the authorized user to make sure the card is always paid on time and maintains low credit utilization (card balance/limit percentage). Otherwise, piggybacking could backfire and result in a worse credit score than you'd have without being an authorized user on the card.

Fortunately, should you discover that the primary account holder is not managing the account to your liking, you can have yourself removed from the account -- preferably by having the primary account holder contact the lender -- and have it removed from your credit report by disputing it as "not mine" with the credit bureaus.

In an attempt to head off such piggybacking abuse, the FICO 8 credit score, launched in 2009, initially excluded accounts held as an authorized user from scoring. FICO quickly reversed course, however, and went back to allowing piggybacking in scores -- but with an adjustment to generate fewer points for accounts held as an authorized user than as a primary account holder. It had become apparent to FICO that the price for discouraging piggybacking abuse by a relative few would be the denial of honestly-earned credit history for millions of legitimate authorized users -- most often the spouses of primary cardholders who use and manage these accounts no differently than those in the primary role.

If your parents or anyone else you know has good credit have them add you to the card.

You should consider the authorized user option as an easy-to-implement, minimal-risk way to build or rebuild credit.

NOTE: You are not merging your whole credit report with someone. Many people are scared because this is what they think. Look the rich have been doing this for a long time. Here is how it works. Little Susan is starting college she has no credit or even bad credit. Her parents have 6 credit cards with perfect payment history for 18 years. They add her as an authorized user on 4 cards with a simple phone call. They don't have credit cards issued so she cant rack up any debt.
Susan all of a sudden has fantastic credit. The credit card companies have this all setup. Most of the time you can login and add the user online and check the box issue a card yes or no.

Pay To Be An Authorized User

NOTE: You can pay to become an Authorized User. There is a whole industry around this business. You have to be extremely careful who you are dealing with. Never deal with a company that also does credit repair. Here is one that is very reputable in this industry.

My Experience: Finance Degree, 6 years loans officer at a national bank, 4 1/2 years credit bureau manager for one of the big three credit bureau's   John Harris

Boostmyscore.net

Years ago, several online companies advertised the ability to add "*Seasoned Primary Tradelines*" to your credit report. These tradelines could look better on your credit report to a mortgage underwriter than a "*Seasoned Authorized User Tradeline*". Since the account would appear in a credit report as being individually managed by the borrower (*Primary*), and because it showed several years of credit history (*Seasoned*), it had the potential to boost the credit score AND trick underwriters into believing it belonged to the applicant. As you can imagine, the "**Seasoned Primary** Tradeline" practice appeared to be fraudulent to many in the law enforcement community. Several businesses advertising that service were quickly sought out and shut down.

Bear in mind that, as opposed to a "*Seasoned Primary Tradeline*", a "*New Primary* Tradeline" (a new credit card account, for example) will most likely cause a drop in your credit score. Your score will typically recover, once the New Primary Tradeline has aged for a couple years.

For these reasons, BoostMyScore does not assist clients with adding "*Seasoned Primary* Tradelines" to their credit report. We also do not assist our clients in applying for "*New Primary*Tradelines."

To be clear, BoostMyScore specializes in the addition of "*Seasoned Authorized User Tradelines*," which continue to deliver an astonishing boost to your **FICO** Score, just as they always have. Guaranteed!

Double All Your Cards

Take all your credit cards that are in good standing as well as your ATM card and call them all in saying you lost your wallet. There are two reasons to do this to your cards. First any recurring charges that keep coming in that you don't know or mean to cancel will not get charged again. Simply reset up whatever you really need on your new card number.

Secondly all the cards will stay on your credit report and the new ones will show up with the same start date. This will double all your good accounts.

Deleting Items From Your Credit Report

NOTE: Ok, Look here is where you have to make a big decision. Do you go it alone or hire someone. Well I am going to be straight up honest with you. Most of the large internet credit repair companies don't do a very good job. Now that being said should you do it yourself? Here is my suggestion. You work on adding credit lines and you have a professional fix your negative items. Now I am going to show you how to fix everything yourself. It's just that the credit bureaus are going to try to mess you up all the way. So before I get into the dispute process I am going to give you an option you should really consider.

There is a company that I have been dealing with for a long time. They are out of Murrieta Ca. They are a husband and wife team with a small staff. They deal with a lot of home buyers looking to buy a property but need some "Credit Repair". If credit repair was an Olympic sport they would get a GOLD Medal. They charge $200 enrollment and many times will email $150 specials. Then its $79 a month for 3 months. So you are talking about approximately $400 over 4 months. They are registered with the Department of Justice and follow strict adherence to State and Federal laws. After the 3 months is over that's all they can do.

If you want to sit back and watch things get deleted from your credit report these are your people. Thank your lucky stars that you found them.

www.dcrusa.com

My Experience: Finance Degree, 6 years loans officer at a national bank, 4 1/2 years credit bureau manager for one of the big three credit bureau's   John Harris

Dedicated Credit Repair is a family owned credit remediation company that has been in operation for over a decade. Founders Jared and Tiffany Hazelaar created DCR's programs out of a desire to help consumers recover from the financial stress and confusion that comes about when a consumer is struggling through credit challenges.

DCR's mission is to help consumers restore their credit integrity by using legal, ethical, and affordable strategies that work quickly. There founders know firsthand the struggle that consumers face when life events such as loss of job, illness, divorce and many other diverse circumstances happen that are out of one's control.

Their faith, coupled with personal experience serve as a catalyst to constantly be improving our programs and technology to accomplish incredible results in the shortest amount of time. Since day one, the company has been registered with the Department of Justice and follows strict adherence to State and Federal laws.

NOTE: They have this great dispute dashboard you can login and see the deletions.

PS: I wouldn't steer you wrong, these guys are fantastic that's why they only have great reviews.

REMEMBER KEEP SAYING "I AM THE PERSON WITH GREAT CREDIT"

Dispute Dashboard

Help for this page:

Select Report:

All Credit Bureaus   ← Change charts here

Repaired & Deleted Items

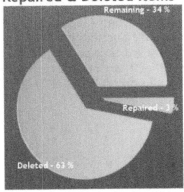

Credit & Dispute Report

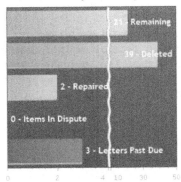

Credit Report Summary

Equifax		Experian		TransUnion	
Start Date:	10/23/2017	Start Date:	10/23/2017	Start Date:	10/23/2017
Total Positive Items:		Total Positive Items:		Total Positive Items:	
Total Negative Items:	21	Total Negative Items:	20	Total Negative Items:	21
Repaired / Deleted to date:	19	Repaired / Deleted to date:	9	Repaired / Deleted to date:	13
Percent Completed:	90%	Percent Completed:	45%	Percent Completed:	62%
Items In Dispute:	0	Items In Dispute:	0	Items In Dispute:	0

Repairing Your Own Credit

3 Reasons You Never Dispute Things Online

I NEED TO SAY THIS AGAIN AND AGAIN NEVER DISPUTE ANYTHING ONLINE.

Reason Number 1: Time

My Experience: Finance Degree, 6 years loans officer at a national bank, 4 1/2 years credit bureau manager for one of the big three credit bureau's   John Harris

One important factor you have on your side when disputing errors in your credit report is time. By law, the credit bureaus have 30 days within receipt of that dispute to properly investigate your claim. However, this only applies to reports other than one obtained for free at Annualcreditreport. In that case, the credit bureaus have 45 days to respond.

Reason Number 2: Shortcut The Process

The Credit Bureaus online dispute system is set up in such a way that when you use it, it makes their job that much easier. The information you put into their limited dispute fields falls right into their electronic verification system. By using their online dispute system (E-OSCAR), **you have no proof of the dispute or a paper trail that certified return receipt requested would give you if you had mailed that dispute.** An important aspect of accelerating the credit recovery process is keeping meticulous records.

If you catch the credit bureaus in violation of the Fair Credit Reporting Act or a collection company in violation of the Fair Debt Collection Practices Act, you'll have the necessary ammunition to beat them in court and clear your good name should you have to go that route.

Reason Number 3 : Revision Not In Your Favor "Verified"

When the Fair Credit Reporting Act was revised by FACTA, they put in a section for "Expedited Dispute Resolution" Section 611a(8), also known as the on-line dispute system. If you read this section, you will notice the following;

Well paragraph 2 is the part that requires the CRA to forward your dispute and all related documentation you provide to the creditor or company furnishing the information to the bureau. Paragraph 6 is the part that requires the CRA to provide you with written results of the re-investigation. And paragraph 7 is the part that requires the CRA to provide you with the method of verification on request by you, the consumer.

So as you can see, by using the CRA'S online disputing system (E-OSCAR), which by the way stands for Electronic Online System for Complete and Accurate Reporting (lol), you wouldn't receive a notice from the credit bureaus telling you that the information you disputed has been verified as accurate, which, by receiving this notice is what allows you to request the method of verification (MOV). The credit bureau then must provide you with this information within 15 days of your request.

As you can see, Method of Verification is another important tool to use and a very important part of accelerating the process of credit recovery should you need to delete an item discovered to be in error, incomplete, or unverifiable during the "Credit Audit and Verification" process. So why would you give these rights up; voluntarily no less?

Additionally, the law is not specific enough and does not say "permanently delete or suppress"; herein lays the problem. The Credit Reporting Agencies (CRA) can "soft delete" a disputed trade line for 30 days and then the trade line can reappear when the furnisher (creditor or collector) reports it again in the next 30 day cycle. This is due to the fact that the CRA's are not required to tell the creditor or collector that you disputed it at all, thanks to the "shall not be required to comply with paragraphs 2" if you decide to dispute an item online. Are you getting all of this?

This is a deceptive system in where you, the Amateur Consumer, think you may have succeeded in your dispute and gotten what is known as a "hard delete", but in fact, it is only temporary. Since the creditor or furnisher of that information does not know the item was deleted, they will mistakenly re-report it and then conveniently, the credit bureau will place the negative item back on your report. And if that isn't bad enough, you lose the hard copy of the investigation results you would otherwise have received and been entitled to if the dispute had been sent via certified mail in the first place.

Again, by disputing in writing, as the FTC states you should on their

My Experience: Finance Degree, 6 years loans officer at a national bank, 4 1/2 years credit bureau manager for one of the big three credit bureau's   John Harris

website, the bureaus might temporarily remove a negative item (soft delete) until the information is verified as true but...if the information is verified to be true, they must then notify you in writing within 5 days of putting the item back on your credit report. If they don't, it's a violation of the FCRA and you could potentially sue them for $1,000.

Listen To The FTC

Look, there's a reason why the FTC states right there on its website that you should dispute EVERY item you think is not accurate, incomplete, or unverifiable on your credit in writing and by certified mail, "return receipt requested"; it's because you are protected as a consumer and by disputing online electronically, you lose many rights under FCRA. So why would you ever do this? So listen to me and the FTC and never dispute online.

What The Credit Bureaus Should Do When They Get A Dispute

An employee at the Credit Bureau receives the dispute and personally reviews it. During this review they gather information and documents in regards to the disputed account by contacting the original creditor or collection agency (Data Furnisher).

The Credit Bureau Employee then reviews copies of original documents like the Credit Application, Billing Statements, Billing and Payment Statements or notes in the account looking for any errors in reporting. If anything is in question they will request proof from the "Data Furnisher."

Once a full investigation has been completed, the Credit Bureau Employee will then update the consumer's account according to the results of the investigation.

Here's What Really Happens When You Dispute

Credit bureaus use "Optical Character Recognition" or OCR which is part of their e-OSCAR system. This technology allows them to scan the consumer's letters and convert them into plain text that can be stored into a database. This way, they can deal with the over 20,000 dispute letters that they receive each day.

Your Credit Has Been Outsourced

Thanks to this technology and overseas outsourcing, credit bureaus have reduced that cost of each dispute from around $4.50 down to around 90 cents.

When the letter is received by the Credit Reporting Agency (Credit Bureau) it's electronically scanned with "Optical Character Recognition" and Matched against a DATABASE or "Boiler Plate" of Dispute Letters commonly used by Credit Repair Companies or found in cheap software programs and Credit Repair Books. If the algorithms find that your letter "matches" one of these letters in their database, your dispute will most likely be flagged as Frivolous, suspicious or it is simply ignored.

No matter who writes the dispute letters or how threatening they are, if the scanned version DOES match that of a "Boiler Plate" dispute letter used thousands of times, the scanned version will then be sent electronically overseas for processing. There, an outsource employee will look at the scanned dispute and assign a 3 digit code (even if it has Multiple pages of detailed documentation supporting the claim). Around 85% of disputes will fall under the same 5 codes.

E-Oscar Explained

e-OSCAR is a web-based, Metro 2 compliant, automated system that enables Data Furnishers (Credit Issuers like Bank of America Visa Credit Card and Collection Agencies like NCO Financial), and Credit Reporting Agencies (CRAs) to create and respond to consumer credit history disputes (the Dispute Letters that you mail to them).

Credit Reporting Agencies (CRAs) include Equifax, Experian, Innovis and TransUnion, their affiliates or Independent Credit Bureaus and

My Experience: Finance Degree, 6 years loans officer at a national bank, 4 1/2 years credit bureau manager for one of the big three credit bureau's   John Harris

Mortgage Reporting Companies. e-OSCAR also provides for Data Furnishers (DFs) to send "out-of-cycle" credit history updates to Credit Reporting Agencies (Equifax, Experian, Innovis and TransUnion).

The system primarily supports Automated Credit Dispute Verification (ACDV) and Automated Universal Data form (AUD) processing as well as a number of related processes that handle registration, subscriber code management and reporting. This system was created to reduce the overhead caused by about 20 thousand dispute letters received by the CRAs every day.

Thru the e-OSCAR system, the dispute processor reads the dispute and classifies it under a dispute code selected from a menu. Of these dispute codes, 85% of disputes fall under the same 5 codes. As you can see in the following chart, more than 50% of the disputes are grouped under the classifications of "Not mine and Account Status" which seem to be the more common mistakes incurred by Credit Reporting Agencies.

E-Oscar Codes

001 Not his/hers.
002 Belongs to another individual with same/similar name.
006 Not aware of collection.

008 Late due to change of address & never received statement.
010 Settlement or partial payments accepted.
012 Claims paid the original creditor
014 Claims paid before collection status.
019 Included in the bankruptcy of another person.
023 Claims account closed.
024 Claims account closed by consumer.
031 Contract cancelled or rescinded.
037 Account included in bankruptcy.
038 Claims active military duty.
039 Insurance claim delayed.
040 Account involved in litigation.
041 Claims victim of natural or declared disaster.
100 Claims account deferred.
101 Not liable for account (i.e., ex-spouse, business).
102 Account reaffirmed or not included in bankruptcy.
103 Claims true identity fraud/account fraudulently opened.
104 Claims account take-over, fraudulent charges made on account.
105 Disputes Dates of Last Payment
106 Disputes present/previous Account Status
107 Disputes Special Comment/Compliance Condition
108 Disputes Account Type or Terms Duration
109 Disputes current balance.
110 Claims company will change.
111 Claims company will delete.
112 Claims inaccurate information.

Thru the e-OSCAR system, the dispute processor reads the dispute and classifies it under a dispute code selected from a menu. Of these dispute codes, 85% of disputes fall under the same 5 codes. As you can see in the following chart, more than 50% of the disputes are grouped under the classifications of "Not mine and Account Status" which seem to be the more common mistakes incurred by Credit Reporting Agencies.

Reasons of Dispute Percentages

Reason of Dispute	% of Disputes
Not Mine	31%
Account Status	21%
Inaccurate Information	17%

My Experience: Finance Degree, 6 years loans officer at a national bank, 4 1/2 years credit bureau manager for one of the big three credit bureau's   John Harris

Account Amounts	9%
Account Closed	7%
Disputes Fall Under Same 5 Codes:	**85%**

Once your dispute is converted to one of the "Standardized Dispute Codes" within the e-OSCAR system, the code is sent via e-OSCAR to the Data Furnisher (the Original Creditor or Collection Agency) using a standardized form known as an Automated Credit Dispute Verification Form (ACDV).

When the data furnisher receives an ACDV thru the e-OSCAR system they should begin an "in-depth" investigation. If the furnisher is a Collection Agency, they should contact the Original Creditor for real documentation on the account, but the data furnisher will never receive nor see all the documentation part of the dispute.

Data Furnishers can receive thousands of disputes a month. e-OSCAR's solution to the problem is to send the Data Furnisher all these disputes in one large file (batch file), all at one time. When the data furnisher receives this file, there are several options for processing the data. One such option is called reply all.

This option allows the data furnisher to select a response like "Account Verified" and apply this response to multiple records in the file with a single click.

Another function called "Auto-Populate" allows the data furnisher to Auto Populate responses of ACDV before submitting them back to the credit bureau via the e-OSCAR system.

You can visit the e-OSCAR website at http://www.e-oscar.org to get all the ugly details.

Great News For You About Disputing

Because of the National Consumer Assistance Plan disputing items on your reports will be easier.

If you've disputed errors on your credit reports before, you know that it can be a pain to do so. NCAP provides more resources and support to consumers disputing items on their credit reports.

The plan is for the bureaus to have an improved dispute resolution process with specially trained employees to review all supporting documentation submitted by consumers for all disputes involving fraud, identity theft or mixed-up information. In cases where a creditor rejects a disputed claim through an electronic system, the bureaus won't automatically accept the decision but will give employees the discretion to reinvestigate the dispute. That's huge.

Reports Have Errors

79 percent of all credit reports contain some type of error - and 25 percent contain such serious errors that those individuals could be denied credit.

Here are other significant findings:

54 percent contained inaccurate personal information such as misspelled names, wrong Social Security numbers, inaccurate birth dates, inaccurate information about a spouse and out of date address. For example, one credit report listed a man's business partner as his spouse.

30 percent listed "closed" accounts as "open." For example, listing a student loan that was paid off years ago as still outstanding. Another report listed several credit cards, a mortgage and an auto loan all as open.

22 percent of reports had the same mortgage or loan listed twice. This mistake often occurs when loans are serviced or sold.

8 percent of reports simply didn't list major credit, loan, mortgage or other accounts that could be used to demonstrate the creditworthiness of a consumer.

These errors can create the appearance of a consumer having "too much" credit available, being over-extended, or not having been a

My Experience: Finance Degree, 6 years loans officer at a national bank, 4 1/2 years credit bureau manager for one of the big three credit bureau's   John Harris

responsible payer of his or her obligations.

The "big three" credit report bureaus - Equifax, Experian and TransUnion - have been in this business for years, so how can they possibly be making all of these mistakes?

Most mistakes can be pinned to your creditors and others providing info to the credit bureaus. As mentioned above, some mistakes happen when credit accounts change hands. Some errors are intentional. The report found that some banks admit to not furnishing bureaus with complete information on customers.

Other mistakes are simply human error. According to a credit bureau industry spokesman, some 30,000 data processors file 4.5 billion updates to credit reports each month, leaving considerable room for errors.

Time To Dispute

You first step is disputing directly with the "Credit Bureaus". Remember your collection accounts and the negative items. Ok so here we go.

Two Means of Disputes

1) Disputing with the credit bureau.
2) Disputing with the collection company/original debtor

You have rights in both these situations. Let's get ready to remove those negative items.

The Secret to Disputing Accounts With The Credit Bureaus

EVERY item you think is not accurate, incomplete, or unverifiable on your credit in writing and by certified mail, "return receipt requested".

Many of the adverse items on a credit report may in fact be true.
So, if you were to dispute the adverse items with a traditional dispute process most of those accounts will be "verified" and will stay on your credit report thus in turn keeping your FICO score down.

That is NOT what you are going to do.

SECTION 609 of the Fair Credit Reporting Act does not care whether the negative account is valid or not. The letter disputes the CRA's right to REPORT the adverse account –

NOT whether or not the adverse account is valid. These letters will request, under SECTION 609 of the Fair Credit Reporting Act, that the CRA's send you a copy of the original contract that you signed – that they are supposed to have.

If they are verifying the account as being valid/correct then they, by law, are supposed to have a copy of that contract to do so. THEY DONT. And since they don't they can't provide you a copy nor can they legally verify the account.

Under the Fair Credit Reporting Act they must provide you a copy if you request it. Since they will not be able to provide you such a document the account will be UNVERIFIED and under Federal Law any UNVERIFIED accounts must be deleted.

Disputing with the Bureaus Must Do's

1) First you should hand write all your letters ok I know this seems like a lot of work but it's worth it. You have to be the customer who is really disputing an item. You are not using a website template. You have hand written your letters.

My Experience: Finance Degree, 6 years loans officer at a national bank, 4 1/2 years credit bureau manager for one of the big three credit bureau's   John Harris

2) All Letters have to be notarized.

3) All letters have to be sent registered mail.

4) All letters have to include your "Identification Form"

Dispute Addresses

Experian's mailing address for dispute requests is:
P.O. Box 4500
Allen, TX 75013

Equifax Information Services LLC
P.O. Box 740256
Atlanta, GA 30374

TransUnion Consumer Solutions
P.O. Box 2000
Chester, PA 19022-2000

Always mail to these addresses.

Include this form with letters to Equifax
http://www.equifax.com/cp/MailInDislcosureRequest.pdf

Include this form with letters to TransUnion
https://www.transunion.com/docs/rev/personal/InvestigationRequest.pdf

REMEMBER KEEP SAYING "I AM THE PERSON WITH GREAT CREDIT"

GENERATION 1.0 LETTER

Your Name
Address
City, State
Zip
SSN: 000-00-0000 | DOB: 1/1/1970

Experian
P.O. Box 4500
Allen, TX 75013

According to the Fair Credit Reporting Section 609 (a)(1)(A), you are required by federal law to verify - through the physical verification of the original signed consumer contract - any and all accounts you post on a credit report.

Otherwise, anyone paying for your reporting services could fax, mail or email in a fraudulent account. I demand to see Verifiable Proof (an original Consumer Contract with my Signature on it) you have on file of the accounts listed below.

Your failure to positively verify these accounts has hurt my ability to obtain credit.

Under the FCRA, unverified accounts must be removed and if you are unable to provide me a copy of verifiable proof, you must remove the accounts listed below.

I demand the following accounts be verified or removed immediately.

Account 1 (AT&T) _____   Account #_____
Account 1 (SPRINT) _____   Account #_____

Please note that I have opted out in writing to your forced arbitration terms and am willing to seek legal relief.
{Print Name}
{Signature}
{Date}

IN WITNESS WHEREOF, the said party has signed and sealed these presents the day and year first above written. Signed, sealed and delivered in the presence of:
{PRINT YOUR NAME HERE} _____ Signature
STATE OF
COUNTY OF
I HEREBY CERTIFY that on this day before me, an officer duly qualified to take acknowledgments, personally appeared
{ YOUR NAME HERE }, who has produced
_____ as identification and who executed the foregoing instrument and he/she acknowledged before me that he/she executed the same.
WITNESS my hand and official seal in the County and State aforesaid this _____ day of _____ 2019.

_____ Notary Public
Printed Name
My commission expires:

-------------------End of Letter.

Identification Form GENERATION LETTER

 **My Experience**: Finance Degree, 6 years loans officer at a national bank, 4 1/2 years credit bureau manager for one of the big three credit bureau's   John Harris

On the bottom of this "ID DOCUMENT"

I declare under penalty of perjury (under the laws of the United States of America) that this identification provide is me
John Doe
Signature
Date

Identification Form Requirements

1) Driver License
2) Social Security card - If you are having difficulty locating your Social Security Card, your most recent W-2 form will be accepted **OR** 1st page of a tax return.
3) Proof of Address **ONLY** If your Driver License does not have your current mailing address on it- Any of the following is acceptable:
   a) Current utility bill
   b) Current cell phone bill
   c) Change of address card from DMV
   d) Voided check
   e) 1st page of a bank statement
   f) Current Lease Agreement
   g) Vehicle registration
   h) Vehicle insurance invoice

Contacting the Bureau Requirements

Send the letter I provide to you
Enclose the Identification Form
Have it notarized
Send it registered mail
Keep copies and keep the mailing receipt

Now Track Your letters

Now your letters are ready to send. You will send your letter WITH TRACKING Certified Mail. This is your proof that CRA's get your letter(s).

This is an absolute must. File all your paperwork

Possible Results

My Experience: Finance Degree, 6 years loans officer at a national bank, 4 1/2 years credit bureau manager for one of the big three credit bureau's   John Harris

When you send your notarized letters to Equifax, TransUnion, and Experian they might try to ignore you.

They might send you a reply saying a suspicious letter was sent on your behalf but has been ignored or may try to intimidate you to stop you from continuing your disputes.

Here are some responses.

"We received a suspicious request regarding your personal credit information that we have determined was not sent by you. We have not taken any action on this request and any future requests made in this manner will not be processed and will not receive a response."

You might also get something like this: "Suspicious requests are taken seriously and reviewed by security personnel who will report deceptive activity, including copies of letters deemed as suspicious, to law enforcement officials and to state or federal regulatory agencies."

They may also ask for proof of your identity and request you mail them such proof.

You have already sent a notarized letter identification form with "I declare under penalty of perjury (under the laws of the United States of America) that this identification provide is me"

All these responses are great for you. They show that the bureaus are not providing information required and the timeline is ticking.

They are trying to scare you.

NOTE: The Credit Bureaus can do absolutely nothing to you legally. Even if you are disputing items that are yours.

REMEMBER KEEP SAYING "I AM THE PERSON WITH GREAT CREDIT"

GENERATION 2.0 LETTER

Your Name
Address
City, State
Zip
SSN: 000-00-0000 | DOB: 1/1/1970

Experian
P.O. Box 4500
Allen, TX 75013

According to the Fair Credit Reporting Section 609 (a)(1)(A), you are required by federal law to verify - through the physical verification of the original signed consumer contract - any and all accounts you post on a credit report.

Otherwise, anyone paying for your reporting services could fax, mail or email in a fraudulent account. I demand to see Verifiable Proof (an original Consumer Contract with my Signature on it) you have on file of the accounts listed below.

Your failure to positively verify these accounts has hurt my ability to obtain credit.

Under the FCRA, unverified accounts must be removed and if you are unable to provide me a copy of verifiable proof, you must remove the accounts listed below. I demand the following accounts be verified or removed immediately.

Account 1 (AT&T) _____ Account #_____
Account 1 (SPRINT) _____ Account #_____

Please note that I have opted out in writing to your forced arbitration terms and am willing to seek legal relief.

{Print Name}
{Signature}
{Date}

IN WITNESS WHEREOF, the said party has signed and sealed these presents the day and year first above written. Signed, sealed and delivered in the presence of:
{PRINT YOUR NAME HERE} _____ Signature
STATE OF
COUNTY OF
I HEREBY CERTIFY that on this day before me, an officer duly qualified to take acknowledgments, personally appeared
{   YOUR   NAME   HERE   },   who   has   produced
_____ as identification and who executed the foregoing instrument and he/she acknowledged before me that he/she executed the same.
    WITNESS my hand and official seal in the County and State aforesaid this _____ day of _____ 2019.

_____ Notary Public
Printed Name
My commission expires:

--------------------End of Letter.

Identification Form GENERATION LETTER

My Experience: Finance Degree, 6 years loans officer at a national bank, 4 1/2 years credit bureau manager for one of the big three credit bureau's   John Harris

On the bottom of this   "ID DOCUMENT"

I declare under penalty of perjury (under the laws of the United States of America) that this identification provide is me
John Doe
Signature
Date

Identification Form Requirements

1) Driver License
2) Social Security card - If you are having difficulty locating your Social Security Card, your most recent W-2 form will be accepted **OR** 1st page of a tax return.
3) Proof of Address **ONLY** If your Driver License does not have your current mailing address on it- Any of the following is acceptable:
   a) Current utility bill
   b) Current cell phone bill
   c) Change of address card from DMV
   d) Voided check
   e) 1st page of a bank statement
   f) Current Lease Agreement
   g) Vehicle registration
   h) Vehicle insurance invoice

Contacting the Bureau Requirements

Send the letter I provide to you
Enclose the Identification Form
Have it notarized
Send it registered mail
Keep copies and keep the mailing receipt

Now Track Your letters

Now your letters are ready to send. You will send your letter WITH TRACKING Certified Mail. This is your proof that CRA's get your letter(s).

This is an absolute must. File all your paperwork

My Experience: Finance Degree, 6 years loans officer at a national bank, 4 1/2 years credit bureau manager for one of the big three credit bureau's   John Harris

GENERATION 3.0 LETTER

Your Name
Address
City, State
Zip
SSN: 000-00-0000 | DOB: 1/1/1970

Experian
P.O. Box 4500
Allen, TX 75013

    Please be advised this is my THIRD WRITTEN REQUEST and FINAL WARNING that I fully intend to pursue litigation in accordance with the FCRA to enforce my rights and seek relief and recover all monetary damages that I may be entitled to under Section 616 and Section 617 regarding your continued willful and negligent noncompliance.
    Despite two written requests, the unverified items listed below still remain on my credit report in violation of Federal Law.
    You are required under the FCRA to have a copy of the original creditors documentation on file to verify that this information is mine and is correct.
    In the results of your first investigation and subsequent reinvestigation, you stated in writing that you "verified" that these items are being "reported correctly" ?
    Who verified these accounts?   You have NOT provided me a copy of ANY original documentation (a consumer contract with my signature on it) as required under Section 609 (a)(1)(A) & Section 611 (a)(1)(A).
    Furthermore you have failed to provide the method of verification as required under Section 611 (a) (7).
    Please be advised that under Section 611 (5)(A) of the FCRA – you are required to "…promptly DELETE all information which cannot be verified."
    The law is very clear as to the Civil liability and the remedy available to me (Section 616 & 617) if you fail to comply with Federal Law. I am a litigious consumer and fully intend on pursuing litigation in this matter to enforce my rights under the FCRA.

Account 1 (AT&T) _____ Account #_____
Account 1 (SPRINT) _____ Account #_____

Please note that I have opted out in writing to your forced arbitration terms and am willing to seek legal relief.

{Print Name}
{Signature}
{Date}

IN WITNESS WHEREOF, the said party has signed and sealed these presents the day and year first above written. Signed, sealed and delivered in the presence of:
{PRINT YOUR NAME HERE} _____ Signature
STATE OF
COUNTY OF
I HEREBY CERTIFY that on this day before me, an officer duly qualified to take acknowledgments, personally appeared
{   YOUR   NAME   HERE   }, who   has   produced _____ as identification and who executed the foregoing instrument and he/she acknowledged before me that he/she executed the same.

REMEMBER KEEP SAYING "I AM THE PERSON WITH GREAT CREDIT"

WITNESS my hand and official seal in the County and State aforesaid this _____ day of _____ 2019.

_____ Notary Public
Printed Name
My commission expires:

---------------------End of Letter.

Identification Form GENERATION LETTER

On the bottom of this "ID DOCUMENT"

I declare under penalty of perjury (under the laws of the United States of America) that this identification provide is me
John Doe
Signature
Date

My Experience: Finance Degree, 6 years loans officer at a national bank, 4 1/2 years credit bureau manager for one of the big three credit bureau's   John Harris

Identification Form Requirements

1) Driver License
2) Social Security card - If you are having difficulty locating your Social Security Card, your most recent W-2 form will be accepted **OR** 1st page of a tax return.
3) Proof of Address **ONLY** If your Driver License does not have your current mailing address on it- Any of the following is acceptable:
   a) Current utility bill
   b) Current cell phone bill
   c) Change of address card from DMV
   d) Voided check
   e) 1st page of a bank statement
   f) Current Lease Agreement
   g) Vehicle registration
   h) Vehicle insurance invoice

Contacting the Bureau Requirements

Send the letter I provide to you
Enclose the Identification Form
Have it notarized
Send it registered mail
Keep copies and keep the mailing receipt

Now Track Your letters

Now your letters are ready to send. You will send your letter WITH TRACKING Certified Mail. This is your proof that CRA's get your letter(s).

This is an absolute must. File all your paperwork

Left Blank Intentionally

My Experience: Finance Degree, 6 years loans officer at a national bank, 4 1/2 years credit bureau manager for one of the big three credit bureau's   John Harris

GENERATION 4.0 LETTER

Your Name
Address
City, State
Zip
SSN: 000-00-0000 | DOB: 1/1/1970

Experian
P.O. Box 4500
Allen, TX 75013

NOTICE OF PENDING LITIGATION SEEKING RELIEF AND MONETARY DAMAGES UNDER FCRA SECTION 616 & SECTION 617 Please accept this final written OFFER OF SETTLEMENT BEFORE LITIGATION as my attempt to amicably resolve your continued violation of the Fair Credit Reporting Act regarding your refusal to delete UNVERIFIED information from my consumer file.

I intend to pursue litigation in accordance with the FCRA to seek relief and recover all monetary damages that I may be entitled to under Section 616 and Section 617 if the UNVERIFIED items listed below are not deleted immediately.

A copy of this letter as well as copies of the three written letters sent to you previously will also become part of a formal complaint to the Federal Trade Commission and shall be used as evidence in pending litigation provided you fail to comply with this offer of settlement. Despite three written requests, the unverified items listed below still remain on my credit report in violation of Federal Law.

You are required under the FCRA to have a copy of the original creditors documentation on file to verify that this information is mine and is correct. In the results of your investigations, you stated in writing that you "verified" that these items are being "reported correctly"? Who verified these accounts?

You have NOT provided me a copy of ANY original documentation (a consumer contract with my signature on it) as required under Section 609 (a)(1)(A) & Section 611 (a)(1)(A).

Furthermore you have failed to provide the method of verification as required under Section 611 (a) (7). Please be advised that under Section 611 (5)(A) of the FCRA – you are required to "…promptly DELETE all information which cannot be verified."

The law is very clear as to the Civil liability and the remedy available to me (Section 616 & 617) if you fail to comply with Federal Law. I am a litigious consumer and fully intend on pursuing litigation in this matter to enforce my rights under the FCRA.

Account 1 (AT&T) _____   Account #_____
Account 1 (SPRINT) _____   Account #_____

Please note that I have opted out in writing to your forced arbitration terms and am willing to seek legal relief.
 {Print Name}
 {Signature}
 {Date}

IN WITNESS WHEREOF, the said party has signed and sealed these presents the day and year first above written. Signed, sealed and delivered in the presence of:
 {PRINT YOUR NAME HERE} _____ Signature
 STATE OF
 COUNTY OF
 I HEREBY CERTIFY that on this day before me, an officer duly qualified to take acknowledgments, personally appeared
 {   YOUR   NAME   HERE   },   who   has   produced

REMEMBER KEEP SAYING "I AM THE PERSON WITH GREAT CREDIT"

_____ as identification and who executed the foregoing instrument and he/she acknowledged before me that he/she executed the same.
    WITNESS my hand and official seal in the County and State aforesaid this _____ day of _____2019.

_____ Notary Public
Printed Name
My commission expires:

---------------------End of Letter.

Identification Form GENERATION LETTER

On the bottom of this "ID DOCUMENT"

I declare under penalty of perjury (under the laws of the United States of America) that this identification provide is me
John Doe
Signature
Date

My Experience: Finance Degree, 6 years loans officer at a national bank, 4 1/2 years credit bureau manager for one of the big three credit bureau's   John Harris

Identification Form Requirements

1) Driver License
2) Social Security card - If you are having difficulty locating your Social Security Card, your most recent W-2 form will be accepted **OR** 1st page of a tax return.
3) Proof of Address **ONLY** If your Driver License does not have your current mailing address on it- Any of the following is acceptable:
    a) Current utility bill
    b) Current cell phone bill
    c) Change of address card from DMV
    d) Voided check
    e) 1st page of a bank statement
    f) Current Lease Agreement
    g) Vehicle registration
    h) Vehicle insurance invoice

Contacting the Bureau Requirements

Send the letter I provide to you
Enclose the Identification Form
Have it notarized
Send it registered mail
Keep copies and keep the mailing receipt

Now Track Your letters

Now your letters are ready to send. You will send your letter WITH TRACKING Certified Mail. This is your proof that CRA's get your letter(s).

This is an absolute must. File all your paperwork

Left Blank Intentionally

My Experience: Finance Degree, 6 years loans officer at a national bank, 4 1/2 years credit bureau manager for one of the big three credit bureau's   John Harris

GENERATION 5.0 LETTER

Your Name
Address
City, State
Zip
SSN: 000-00-0000 | DOB: 1/1/1970

Experian
P.O. Box 4500
Allen, TX 75013

NOTICE OF PENDING LITIGATION SEEKING RELIEF AND MONETARY DAMAGES UNDER FCRA SECTION 616 & SECTION 617 Please accept this final written OFFER OF SETTLEMENT BEFORE LITIGATION as my attempt to amicably resolve your continued violation of the Fair Credit Reporting Act regarding your refusal to delete UNVERIFIED information from my consumer file.

I intend to pursue litigation in accordance with the FCRA to seek relief and recover all monetary damages that I may be entitled to under Section 616 and Section 617 if the UNVERIFIED items listed below are not deleted immediately.

A copy of this letter as well as copies of the three written letters sent to you previously will also become part of a formal complaint to the Federal Trade Commission and shall be used as evidence in pending litigation provided you fail to comply with this offer of settlement. Despite three written requests, the unverified items listed below still remain on my credit report in violation of Federal Law.

You are required under the FCRA to have a copy of the original creditors documentation on file to verify that this information is mine and is correct. In the results of your investigations, you stated in writing that you "verified" that these items are being "reported correctly"?   Who verified these accounts?
You have NOT provided me a copy of ANY original documentation (a consumer contract with my signature on it) as required under Section 609 (a)(1)(A) & Section 611 (a)(1)(A).
Furthermore you have failed to provide the method of verification as required under Section 611 (a) (7).   Please be advised that under Section 611 (5)(A) of the FCRA – you are required to "...promptly DELETE all information which cannot be verified."
The law is very clear as to the Civil liability and the remedy available to me (Section 616 & 617) if you fail to comply with Federal Law. I am a litigious consumer and fully intend on pursuing litigation in this matter to enforce my rights under the FCRA.
Account 1 (AT&T) _____   Account #_____
Account 1 (SPRINT) _____   Account #_____

If I don't get proper documentation I will be filling my complaint at:
www.consumerfinance.gov/Complaint/
and
www.ftccomplaintassistant.gov/
Please note that I have opted out in writing to your forced arbitration terms and am willing to seek legal relief.
{Print Name}
{Signature}
{Date}
IN WITNESS WHEREOF, the said party has signed and sealed these presents the day and year first above written. Signed, sealed and delivered in the presence of:

REMEMBER KEEP SAYING "I AM THE PERSON WITH GREAT CREDIT"

{PRINT YOUR NAME HERE} _____ Signature
STATE OF
COUNTY OF
I HEREBY CERTIFY that on this day before me, an officer duly qualified to take acknowledgments, personally appeared
{ YOUR NAME HERE }, who has produced _____ as identification and who executed the foregoing instrument and he/she acknowledged before me that he/she executed the same.
WITNESS my hand and official seal in the County and State aforesaid this _____ day of _____2019.

_____ Notary Public
Printed Name
My commission expires:

Identification Form GENERATION LETTER

On the bottom of this "ID DOCUMENT"

I declare under penalty of perjury (under the laws of the United States of America) that this identification provide is me
John Doe
Signature
Date

My Experience: Finance Degree, 6 years loans officer at a national bank, 4 1/2 years credit bureau manager for one of the big three credit bureau's   John Harris

Identification Form Requirements

1) Driver License
2) Social Security card - If you are having difficulty locating your Social Security Card, your most recent W-2 form will be accepted **OR** 1st page of a tax return.
3) Proof of Address **ONLY** If your Driver License does not have your current mailing address on it- Any of the following is acceptable:
   a) Current utility bill
   b) Current cell phone bill
   c) Change of address card from DMV
   d) Voided check
   e) 1st page of a bank statement
   f) Current Lease Agreement
   g) Vehicle registration
   h) Vehicle insurance invoice

Contacting the Bureau Requirements

Send the letter I provide to you
Enclose the Identification Form
Have it notarized
Send it registered mail
Keep copies and keep the mailing receipt

Now Track Your letters

Now your letters are ready to send. You will send your letter WITH TRACKING Certified Mail. This is your proof that CRA's get your letter(s).

This is an absolute must. File all your paperwork

Small Claims Form Included

With this 6th letter enclose a copy of a small claims court filling. **Fill it out completely like you are ready to file it.**

Now don't actually file it just fill it out. You can get one for free at your local court house. Name the bureau as the defendant.

What you file against them for:

negligent and willful failure to provide - through the physical verification of the original signed consumer contract - any and all accounts you post on a credit report.
In violation Section 609 (a)(1)(A), FCRA

negligent and willful failure to reinvestigate the disputed entries in violation of sections 611(a), 616, and 617 of the FCRA, 15 U.S.C. §§ 1681i(a), 1681n, 1681o"

My Experience: Finance Degree, 6 years loans officer at a national bank, 4 1/2 years credit bureau manager for one of the big three credit bureau's   John Harris

GENERATION 6.0 LETTER

Your Name
Address
City, State
Zip
SSN: 000-00-0000 | DOB: 1/1/1970
Experian
P.O. Box 4500
Allen, TX 75013

NOTICE OF PENDING LITIGATION SEEKING RELIEF AND MONETARY DAMAGES UNDER FCRA SECTION 616 & SECTION 617 Please accept this final written OFFER OF SETTLEMENT BEFORE LITIGATION as my attempt to amicably resolve your continued violation of the Fair Credit Reporting Act regarding your refusal to delete UNVERIFIED information from my consumer file.

I intend to pursue litigation in accordance with the FCRA to seek relief and recover all monetary damages that I may be entitled to under Section 616 and Section 617 if the UNVERIFIED items listed below are not deleted immediately.

A copy of this letter as well as copies of the three written letters sent to you previously will also become part of a formal complaint to the Federal Trade Commission and shall be used as evidence in pending litigation provided you fail to comply with this offer of settlement. Despite three written requests, the unverified items listed below still remain on my credit report in violation of Federal Law.

You are required under the FCRA to have a copy of the original creditors documentation on file to verify that this information is mine and is correct. In the results of your investigations, you stated in writing that you "verified" that these items are being "reported correctly"? Who verified these accounts?

You have NOT provided me a copy of ANY original documentation (a consumer contract with my signature on it) as required under Section 609 (a)(1)(A) & Section 611 (a)(1)(A).

Furthermore you have failed to provide the method of verification as required under Section 611 (a) (7). Please be advised that under Section 611 (5)(A) of the FCRA – you are required to "…promptly DELETE all information which cannot be verified."

The law is very clear as to the Civil liability and the remedy available to me (Section 616 & 617) if you fail to comply with Federal Law. I am a litigious consumer and fully intend on pursuing litigation in this matter to enforce my rights under the FCRA.

Account 1 (AT&T) _____   Account #_____
Account 1 (SPRINT) _____   Account #_____

If I don't get proper documentation I will be filling my complaint at:
www.consumerfinance.gov/Complaint/
and
www.ftccomplaintassistant.gov/

Please note that I have opted out in writing to your forced arbitration terms and am willing to seek legal relief.

{Print Name}
{Signature}
{Date}

REMEMBER KEEP SAYING "I AM THE PERSON WITH GREAT CREDIT"

IN WITNESS WHEREOF, the said party has signed and sealed these presents the day and year first above written. Signed, sealed and delivered in the presence of:

{PRINT YOUR NAME HERE} _____ Signature

STATE OF
COUNTY OF

I HEREBY CERTIFY that on this day before me, an officer duly qualified to take acknowledgments, personally appeared { YOUR NAME HERE }, who has produced _____ as identification and who executed the foregoing instrument and he/she acknowledged before me that he/she executed the same.

WITNESS my hand and official seal in the County and State aforesaid this _____ day of _____2019.

_____ Notary Public
Printed Name
My commission expires:

Identification Form GENERATION LETTER

On the bottom of this "ID DOCUMENT"

I declare under penalty of perjury (under the laws of the United States of America) that this identification provide is me
John Doe
Signature

My Experience: Finance Degree, 6 years loans officer at a national bank, 4 1/2 years credit bureau manager for one of the big three credit bureau's   John Harris

Date

Identification Form Requirements

1) Driver License
2) Social Security card - If you are having difficulty locating your Social Security Card, your most recent W-2 form will be accepted **OR** 1st page of a tax return.
3) Proof of Address **ONLY** If your Driver License does not have your current mailing address on it- Any of the following is acceptable:
   a) Current utility bill
   b) Current cell phone bill
   c) Change of address card from DMV
   d) Voided check
   e) 1st page of a bank statement
   f) Current Lease Agreement
   g) Vehicle registration
   h) Vehicle insurance invoice

Contacting the Bureau Requirements

Send the letter I provide to you
Enclose the Identification Form
Have it notarized
Send it registered mail
Keep copies and keep the mailing receipt

Now Track Your letters

Now your letters are ready to send. You will send your letter WITH TRACKING Certified Mail. This is your proof that CRA's get your letter(s).

This is an absolute must. File all your paperwork

Filling Your Complaint

You will have file complaint here:

www.consumerfinance.gov/Complaint/

www.ftccomplaintassistant.gov/

NOTE: The "Credit Bureaus" will never ignore a complaint from these organizations.

Scan all your documents sent to the bureaus and their responses. You will be able to upload them. Make sure you send ALL DOCUMENTS AND THE TIME LINE.

My Experience: Finance Degree, 6 years loans officer at a national bank, 4 1/2 years credit bureau manager for one of the big three credit bureau's   John Harris

Disputing With The Original Debtor

BEFORE DISPUTING WITH THE ORIGINAL CREDITOR YOU MUST HAVE DISPUTED WITH THE CREDIT BUREAUS .

How to Dispute Listing with Original Creditor

Creditors are the companies who initially reported your account to the credit bureaus and many times they have no record of your account at all. By law they have to remove your account if this is the case and have no proof.

Here is the exact statute in the FCRA:

§ 623. (a)(8) ABILITY OF CONSUMER TO DISPUTE INFORMATION DIRECTLY WITH FURNISHER

(A) IN GENERAL The Federal banking agencies, the National Credit Union Administration, and the Commission shall jointly prescribe regulations that shall identify the circumstances under which a furnisher shall be required to reinvestigate a dispute concerning the accuracy of information contained in a consumer report on the consumer, based on a direct request of a consumer.

(B) CONSIDERATIONS - In prescribing regulations under subparagraph (A), the agencies shall weigh--

(i) the benefits to consumers with the costs on furnishers and the credit reporting system;

(ii) the impact on the overall accuracy and integrity of consumer reports of any such requirements;

(iii) whether direct contact by the consumer with the furnisher would likely result in the most expeditious resolution of any such dispute; and

(iv) the potential impact on the credit reporting process if credit repair organizations, as defined in section 403(3), including entities that would be a credit repair organization, but for section 403(3)(B)(i), are able to circumvent the prohibition in subparagraph (G).

(C) APPLICABILITY Subparagraphs (D) through (G) shall apply in any circumstance identified under the regulations promulgated under subparagraph (A).

(D) SUBMITTING A NOTICE OF DISPUTE- A consumer who seeks to dispute the accuracy of information shall provide a dispute notice directly to such person at the address specified by the person for such notices that--

(i) identifies the specific information that is being disputed;

(ii) explains the basis for the dispute; and

(iii) includes all supporting documentation required by the furnisher to substantiate the basis of the dispute.

(E) DUTY OF PERSON AFTER RECEIVING NOTICE OF DISPUTE- After receiving a notice of dispute from a consumer pursuant to subparagraph (D), the person that provided the information in dispute to a consumer reporting agency shall--

(i) conduct an investigation with respect to the disputed information;

(ii) review all relevant information provided by the consumer with the notice;

(iii) complete such person's investigation of the dispute and report the results of the investigation to the consumer before the expiration of the period under section 611(a)(1) within which a consumer reporting agency would be required to complete its action if the consumer had elected to dispute the information under that section; and

(iv) if the investigation finds that the information reported was inaccurate, promptly notify each consumer reporting agency to which the person furnished the inaccurate information of that determination and provide to the agency any correction to that information that is necessary to make the information provided by the person accurate.

(F) FRIVOLOUS OR IRRELEVANT DISPUTE-

(i) IN GENERAL- This paragraph shall not apply if the person receiving a notice of a dispute from a consumer reasonably determines that the dispute is frivolous or irrelevant, including--

(I) by reason of the failure of a consumer to provide sufficient information to investigate the disputed information; or

(II) the submission by a consumer of a dispute that is substantially the same as a dispute previously submitted by or for the consumer, either directly to the person or through a consumer reporting agency under subsection (b), with respect to which the person has already performed the person's duties under this paragraph or subsection (b), as applicable.

(ii) NOTICE OF DETERMINATION - Upon making any determination under clause (i) that a dispute is frivolous or irrelevant, the person shall notify the consumer of such determination not later than 5 business days

My Experience: Finance Degree, 6 years loans officer at a national bank, 4 1/2 years credit bureau manager for one of the big three credit bureau's John Harris

after making such determination, by mail or, if authorized by the consumer for that purpose, by any other means available to the person.

(iii) CONTENTS OF NOTICE - A notice under clause (ii) shall include-

(I) the reasons for the determination under clause (i); and

(II) identification of any information required to investigate the disputed information, which may consist of a standardized form describing the general nature of such information.

and

§ 623. (b) Duties of furnishers of information upon notice of dispute.

(1) In general. After receiving notice pursuant to section 611(a)(2) [§ 1681i] of a dispute with regard to the completeness or accuracy of any information provided by a person to a consumer reporting agency, the person shall

(A) conduct an investigation with respect to the disputed information;

(B) review all relevant information provided by the consumer reporting agency pursuant to section 611(a)(2) [§ 1681i];

(C) report the results of the investigation to the consumer reporting agency;

(D) if the investigation finds that the information is incomplete or inaccurate, report those results to all other consumer reporting agencies to which the person furnished the information and that compile and maintain files on consumers on a nationwide basis; and

(E) if an item of information disputed by a consumer is found to be inaccurate or incomplete or cannot be verified after any reinvestigation under paragraph (1), for purposes of reporting to a consumer reporting agency only, as appropriate, based on the results of the reinvestigation promptly --

(i) modify that item of information;

(ii) delete that item of information; or

(iii) permanently block the reporting of that item of information.

In Layman's Terms

Now that your head is spinning with all that law, here is what is really means.

Basically, you can dispute information placed on your credit report by an original creditor in the same way as you would with a credit bureau. An original creditor must do the following.

Conduct an investigation of the dispute.

Review all information provided by the consumer relating to the dispute.

Respond within 30 days to the investigation.

If the information is inaccurate, they must notify the credit bureaus of the mistake and tell the credit bureau to correct it.

However, the creditor can also determine the dispute is frivolous just like a credit bureau can. Some reasons as to why a dispute may be frivolous.

You just disputed the same thing without changing the reason for the dispute.

You haven't provided enough information for the creditor to conduct an investigation. At the minimum, you need to identify the account by account number and provide a reason why you are disputing.

If the creditor does determine the dispute is frivolous, they must notify you in writing by any other means available to the person within 5 days.

If the Creditor Fails to Comply with the Law

If the original creditor fails to comply with your dispute, they are in violation of the FCRA, but you can't sue them unless you have disputed with the Credit Bureaus first.

Disputing with the credit bureau first is not something you can shortcut or forget. In order to place the liability of reporting accurately squarely on the shoulders of the creditor, you must have disputed the listing with the credit bureaus. This in writing, disputed a listing with the credit bureaus and then WAITED FOR THE RESULTS OF THE INVESTIGATION.

Here is the law which enforces the fact that you must dispute with the credit bureau first:

§ 623. (c) LIMITATION ON LIABILITY- Except as provided in section 621(c)(1)(B), sections 616 and 617 do not apply to any violation of--

(1) subsection (a) of this section, including any regulations issued thereunder;

(2) subsection (e) of this section, except that nothing in this paragraph shall limit, expand, or otherwise affect liability under section 616 or 617, as applicable, for violations of subsection (b) of this section;

Sections 616 and 617 of the FCRA talk about how much the fines are for violations of the FCRA (the willful and negligent non-compliance), typically $1,000.

What the above section of the FCRA § 623(c) means is that if you dispute with the original creditors first, without having disputing through the credit bureaus, and they refuse to answer you, or provide you with proof, yes, they are in violation of the FCRA, but you as a private citizen cannot take them to court and sue them; only your state authorities (like your state attorney general) or federal authorities (like the FTC) can sue them.

However, if you have disputed the information with the credit bureaus first, they are supposed to have talked to the original creditor, even though we know that doesn't happen, and the original creditor is supposed to have at that time conducted an investigation, under FCRA §

My Experience: Finance Degree, 6 years loans officer at a national bank, 4 1/2 years credit bureau manager for one of the big three credit bureau's   John Harris

623(b), under which you, as a private citizen can sue them. When you go to the original creditor under FCRA § 623(a)(8), you are just merely asking for the OC's proof that they must have provided to the credit bureaus during the OC's thorough investigation. If they have no proof of negative information, but the credit bureau says that the results of the investigation show the negative information is accurate, then you have the OC on an actionable, sue-able (by you) offense.

Once again, YOU MUST DISPUTE WITH THE CREDIT BUREAUS FIRST

Steps to Dispute With Original Creditor

What is the exact procedure when you want to dispute things with the original creditor?

The Steps:
Dispute the listing with the credit bureau.
Wait for the results of the investigation.
If the listing is deleted or modified per your desires, you're done!
If not send this letter.

REMEMBER KEEP SAYING "I AM THE PERSON WITH GREAT CREDIT"

Letter to the Original Debtor

Your Name
Address
City, State
Zip
SSN: 000-00-0000 | DOB: 1/1/1970

Bank of America
P.O. Box 4568
Dallas, TX 75013

Dear Legal Department:

Re: Acct #XXXXXXXX

This letter is in regards to a phone call I placed to your company regarding the account listed above on <Insert Date>.

I called to inquire about this account that is listed on my Credit Reports. I spoke to **<Insert Customer Service Representative named>** and her employee number is **<Insert #>**, as provided by her. She informed me that your company does not have any information on this account that it was all sent to a collection agency. How did you investigate this account without any documentation? I contacted the collection agency your rep told me about and they could not validate the debt. This collection agency subsequently removed all information regarding this account from my credit reports. If this incorrect information is not removed from my credit reports, I will file suit against your company.

First Name

Last Name

Email

Phone

Zip Code

IN WITNESS WHEREOF, the said party has signed and sealed these presents the day and year first above written. Signed, sealed and delivered in the presence of:
 {PRINT YOUR NAME HERE} _____ Signature
 STATE OF

My Experience: Finance Degree, 6 years loans officer at a national bank, 4 1/2 years credit bureau manager for one of the big three credit bureau's   John Harris

COUNTY OF
I HEREBY CERTIFY that on this day before me, an officer duly qualified to take acknowledgments, personally appeared
    {   YOUR   NAME   HERE   },   who   has   produced
_____ as identification and who executed the foregoing instrument and he/she acknowledged before me that he/she executed the same.
    WITNESS my hand and official seal in the County and State aforesaid this _____ day of _____2016.

_____ Notary Public
Printed Name
My commission expires:

Identification Form

On the bottom of this   "ID DOCUMENT"

REMEMBER KEEP SAYING "I AM THE PERSON WITH GREAT CREDIT"

I declare under penalty of perjury (under the laws of the United States of America) that this identification provide is me
John Doe
Signature
Date

Identification Form Requirements

1) Driver License
2) Social Security card - If you are having difficulty locating your Social Security Card, your most recent W-2 form will be accepted **OR** 1st page of a tax return.
3) Proof of Address **ONLY** If your Driver License does not have your current mailing address on it- Any of the following is acceptable:
    a) Current utility bill
    b) Current cell phone bill
    c) Change of address card from DMV
    d) Voided check
    e) 1st page of a bank statement
    f) Current Lease Agreement
    g) Vehicle registration
    h) Vehicle insurance invoice

Contacting the Bureau Requirements

Send the letter I provide to you
Enclose the Identification Form
Have it notarized
Send it registered mail
Keep copies and keep the mailing receipt

Now Track Your letters

My Experience: Finance Degree, 6 years loans officer at a national bank, 4 1/2 years credit bureau manager for one of the big three credit bureau's   John Harris

Now your letters are ready to send. You will send your letter WITH TRACKING Certified Mail. This is your proof that CRA's get your letter(s).

This is an absolute must. File all your paperwork

Last Option Pay For Deletion Letter

Oliver Rodriguez
123 Main Street, Anytown, CA 12345 · 555-555-5555 · oliver.rodriguez@email.com

September 1, 2018

James Lee
Collection Manager
Bay City Collectors
123 Business Rd.
Business City, NY 54321

Re: Account Number 1234-5678-8765-4321

Dear Mr. Lee:

This letter is in response to your **[letter / call / credit report entry]** on **[date]** related to the debt referenced above. I wish to save us both some time and effort by settling this debt.

Please be aware that this is not an acknowledgment or acceptance of the debt, as I have not received any verification of the debt. Nor is this a promise to pay and is not a payment agreement unless you provide a response as detailed below.

I am aware that your company has the ability to report this debt to the credit bureaus as you deem necessary. Furthermore, you have the ability to change the listing since you are the information furnisher.

I am willing to pay **[this debt in full / $XXX as settlement for this debt]** in return for your agreement to remove all information regarding this debt from the credit reporting agencies within ten calendar days of payment. If you agree to the terms, I will send certified payment in the amount of **$XXX** payable to Bay City Collectors in exchange to have all information related to this debt removed from all of my credit files.

REMEMBER KEEP SAYING "I AM THE PERSON WITH GREAT CREDIT"

If you accept this offer, you also agree not to discuss the offer with any third-party, excluding the original creditor. If you accept the offer, please prepare a letter on your company letterhead agreeing to the terms. This letter should be signed by an authorized agent of Bay City Collectors. The letter will be treated as a contract and subject to the laws of my state.

As granted by the Fair Debt Collection Practices Act, I have the right to dispute this alleged debt. If I do not receive your postmarked response within 15 days, I will withdraw the offer and request full verification of this debt.

Please forward your agreement to the address listed above. Sincerely, Your Name.

Sincerely,

Oliver Rodriguez

Final Note

NOTE: If you don't get everything you wanted deleted contact DCR Credit Repair.

John Harris

www.dcrusa.com

Dedicated Credit Repair is a family owned credit remediation company that has been in operation for over a decade. Founders Jared and Tiffany Hazelaar created DCR's programs out of a desire to help consumers recover from the financial stress and confusion that comes about when a consumer is struggling through credit challenges.

DCR's mission is to help consumers restore their credit integrity by using legal, ethical, and affordable strategies that work quickly. There founders know firsthand the struggle that consumers face when life events such as loss of job, illness, divorce and many other diverse circumstances happen that are out of one's control.

Their faith, coupled with personal experience serve as a catalyst to constantly be improving our programs and technology to accomplish incredible results in the shortest amount of time. Since day one, the company has been registered with the Department of Justice and follows strict adherence to State and Federal laws.

My Experience: Finance Degree, 6 years loans officer at a national bank, 4 1/2 years credit bureau manager for one of the big three credit bureau's   John Harris

Made in the USA
Middletown, DE
08 March 2019